"If you are ready to fly high in health, h[...] [...]f living, read my friend Calvin's book, containing the secret tips, tricks and techniques for living a magnificent life."

- Mark Victor Hansen – Bestselling Author: *Chicken Soup For The Soul*

"I loved reading this book. The authors share many beautiful truths, an abundance of inspiration, and numerous powerful lessons you will use immediately to improve the quality of your life. Give a copy to those you love."

- Bob Proctor – Bestselling Author: *You Were Born Rich*

"Flying High is a true story of undeniable inspiration. The book is enriching and enlightening, a definite must read. Flying High gives us all hope through the true life stories of two extraordinary individuals who have overcome so much, and generously share the lessons they have learned along the way . . ."

- Raymond Moody, MD, PhD – Bestselling Author: *Life After Life*

"If you are struggling with adversity of any kind, whether sickness, financial, or just trying to figure out your purpose in this world, there's something precious in this story for you—a powerful dose of inspiration that will encourage you along your own journey. And if you simply want to experience a real-life ride from earthbound living, to the limitless potentials of God's open skies, then Flying High will put a song in your heart and take you soaring."

- Naomi Judd – Five time Grammy Award winning singer/songwriter; Member of Country Music duo *The Judds*

"This rare book combines success principles, motivational insights and spiritual self-help teachings that are bound together beautifully in a true story of overcoming adversity. It truly earns the right to be called a body, mind & spirit masterpiece."

- Betty J. Eadie – Bestselling Author:
Embraced By The Light

"Calvin, Your story is powerful and most inviting . . . anything I say about it is the equivalent of attempting to gild an already beautiful lily. The book will do well."

- Astronaut Edgar Mitchell – President:
Institute of Noetic Sciences

"FLYING HIGH is a great inspiration for anyone who faces the life and death struggle of someone they cherish. It is a universal and eternal love story—of the love between husbands and wives, parents and children, and compassionate friends—and the fight for their beloved to continue living long enough to realize their purpose and their dreams. You will find enormous comfort reading this book."

- Dannion Brinkley – Bestselling Author:
Saved By The Light

You'll love this insightful book! Not only is it a great story, but the lessons within its pages will help you in facing challenges as you strive to fly higher yourself. Don't wait until everything is just right—there will always be obstacles in your path. So what? With each step you take you'll grow stronger. Always remember, it costs nothing to dream, but everything not to...

- Rita Davenport – Author, Speaker,
Entrepreneur & TV Host

"As one who believes in "signs" from above, I have fallen in love with this touching and beautiful book! The unique way in which it came to be, the two fellow travelers who found answers in unlikely places, the strange and lovely examples of heavenly timing—could Anyone but God have designed all of this? Readers who are looking for answers in this muddled world, and that's probably all of us, will love FLYING HIGH."

- Joan Wester Anderson – Bestselling
Author: *Where Angels Walk*

Flying High is a trip home - home to the native Tennessee I've never left and to the friends and colleagues who have made it rich for a whole nation with song and color and story. But Flying High is about a state of mind, as well, about a way of being, about a sureness of believing that is native to us all, if only we will claim it. Read with joy and see for yourself what is and what can be.

- Phyllis Tickle – Founding Religion Editor:
Publisher's Weekly & Author: *The Shaping
of a Life: A Spiritual Landscape*

"I really loved the book. I couldn't put it down. I started reading it before my surgery; I read it all the way to the time they rolled me into the surgery room! And then I picked it right back up as soon as I was conscious again. What a beautiful story, woven with so many life-altering lessons, and the ending gave me goose bumps :-). Thank You for sharing this beautiful book with us."

- Sandy Gallagher – President/CEO
LifeSuccess Group of Companies

"What a great book! I've known these spiritual principles for years... but actually seeing them put to the test through Stowe's incredible journey, and Calvin's amazing life... I am moved, inspired, and recharged!"

- Karen Taylor-Good – Motivational
Speaker & Grammy-nominated
singer/songwriter: *How Can I Help
You Say Goodbye?*

flying high

a true story of shared inspiration

Calvin LeHew &
Stowe Dailey Shockey

Published by Outside the BLOX Media, PO Box 864, Franklin, Tenn. 37065

Published in association with Balboa Press, Bloomington, Indiana
and Scribe Book Company, Franklin, Tenn.

Balboa Press books may be ordered through booksellers or by contacting:
Balboa Press
A Division of Hay House
1663 Liberty Drive
Bloomington, IN 47403
www.balboapress.com
1-(877) 407-4847

ISBN: 978-1-4525-3453-4 (sc)
ISBN: 978-1-4525-3455-8 (hc)
ISBN: 978-1-4525-3454-1 (e)

Library of Congress Control Number: 2011906244

Library of Congress Cataloging-in-Publication
Calvin Lehew, Stowe Dailey Shockey
    flying high, a true story of shared inspiration / foreword by Naomi Judd

Printed in the United States of America

Unless otherwise indicated, scripture quotations are taken from New International Version ®
(NIV®). Copyright © 1973, 1978, 1984 by International Bible Society. Used by permission of
Zondervan. All rights reserved.
The King James Version of the Bible (KJV). Public domain.
The Holy Bible, New Living Translation® (nlt®). Copyright © 1996. Used by permission
of Tyndale House Publishers, Inc., Wheaton, Illinois 60189. All rights reserved.

Book Design: Birdsong Creative, Franklin, TN., www.birdsongcreative.com
Cover Photo: Gene Smith

Balboa Press rev date: 7/26/2011

FROM STOWE:

*This book is lovingly dedicated
to my best friend—Peter Shockey—
an answer to prayer.*

....

FROM CALVIN:

*To my wife, Marilyn and
our dogs, Pete and Lucy*

contents

foreword by Naomi Judd

My own life's shown me, it's not what happens to us, it's what we choose to do about it. So, I believe in looking for positive opportunities in every situation—even in crisis. Especially in crisis! The word crisis in Chinese is made up of two characters: danger and opportunity. This uplifting book, written by Calvin LeHew and Stowe Dailey Shockey, weaves the rags-to riches story of Calvin's choices alongside Stowe's heartrending health crisis, which synchronistically unfolded during the writing of the book. Full of thought provoking insights, it is at times poignant and amusing, and always inspirational.

I can't remember not knowing Calvin LeHew. First, through our local restaurants he and his wife Marilyn owned—Miss Daisy's Tearoom (where Wynonna used to wait tables) and Choices Restaurant—they set in motion the wonderful revitalization of our beloved Franklin Tennessee. My family spent many happy times around those festive tables and along the way the LeHews and the Judds developed a deep respect and mutual admiration. I witnessed firsthand how Calvin's faith and positive attitude released boundless energy for making his own dreams into reality—then also for others.

Later we became neighbors in the beautiful rolling hills of Tennessee. On any given day, I might look up and see Calvin flying one of his small ultra light planes or his experimental helicopter over the countryside, trying to reach his desired "higher perspective." If you are fortunate enough to live in Franklin or nearby Leipers Fork, you benefit from this soft-spoken country gentleman, whose visionary projects consciously raised the quality of life.

Finally, I'm proud to call him friend. We share a respect for our beloved land and it's heritage, for dogs, humor and consciousness-raising. A natural born storyteller, Calvin is eager to share colorful lessons of success he's learned along the scenic path of life. In fact, I've wondered more than once when he might write about his insights.

When I heard he co-authored a book called Flying High, I imagined it would be filled with down home wisdom mixed with inspirational philosophy. I knew he was capable of a grits'n'gravy version of The Secret or the writings of Eckhart Tolle. But as I dug deeper, I discovered a far more heart-touching true story of how Calvin's teachings affected his co-writer, Stowe Shockey, in the middle of her own worst nightmare with cancer.

I'm all too familiar with how a life threatening illness can spin your head around, like a tornado ripping through your career, family, and feelings—leaving everything in hopeless disarray. Unexpectedly, while helping compile Calvin's life story, Stowe's health took a horrible turn. But there was Calvin, like a prescription for hope sent ahead, lending a listening ear and firsthand view from his own cancer experience the previous year.

Like myself, you'll be drawn into this very personal and beautiful story, first on account of the remarkable life of the original storyteller. Then, you'll have ah-ha moments of what can happen to us when we wrestle for control of the rudder that steers us between fear and hope.

Calvin often quotes, "what you think about, you bring about"— nothing will change until you change the way you are thinking. And even when you can't change the way things are, you still have the power to choose your reactions. What most of us don't realize is exactly how creative our thoughts can be, whether they're positive or negative. And for creative thinkers like Stowe, and really any of us, the imagination is a wild stallion that we either master, or are trampled by.

If you are struggling with adversity of any kind, whether sickness, financial, or just trying to figure out your purpose in this world, there's something precious in this story for you—a powerful dose of inspiration that will encourage you along your own journey. And if you simply want to experience a real-life ride from earthbound living, to the limitless potentials of God's open skies, then Flying High will put a song in your heart and take you soaring.

—NAOMI JUDD

foreword by Rita Davenport

I was raised in poverty in the South and often told, "Don't try to get above your raising. Don't get your hopes up . . . " they said. "Nobody in this family ever amounted to anything." They weren't exactly encouraging words. Meeting Calvin LeHew and being exposed to his teachings helped me break through those limiting beliefs. He helped give me the confidence I needed to make an impact on the world. I learned that the books we read, the people we meet, the training we receive from seminars, lectures, and studying successful people make all the difference. Your mind is more powerful than you think! And Calvin taught me to guard it carefully.

From the day we met, I recognized Calvin as a kindred spirit, someone who aspires to inspire others. He introduced me to some great teachers, and authors—people like Earl Nightingale, Norman Vincent Peale, Cavett Robert, Og Mandino, Napoleon Hill, and many others who shared priceless success principles with me. (Through Calvin, I even got to meet Earl Nightingale and Norman Vincent Peale!)

Years ago, I hosted a daily TV talk show. It was Calvin who suggested that my life would improve in accordance with the positive programming I received from the famous people I interviewed. And, it did. Consciously applying his teachings, I realized that everyone has a purpose, and the necessary skills and talents to fulfill that purpose. I discovered that "desire," "belief," and "imagination" were the seeds of greatness.

Calvin has been a good friend. But more than that, he has inspired me and taught me many essential keys to success. He gave me the strength to stay on course, keep calm, and carry on when others did not share my passion and vision.

Reading this book was an emotional experience for me. I was reminded once again of the many wonderful principles I've learned over the years from this great teacher. And now, through Calvin's work, thousands of others will be able to discover some of the principles for living a fulfilling life.

Isn't it time for you to realize your greatness and live an abundant life? In today's global world of business, it is more important than ever to find our major purpose—not just for ourselves—but for others. Working with like-minded individuals, we can discover our greatest talents and passions to fulfill our purpose in life for the good of others. Calvin taught me, "It's not about YOU!"

Calvin's life is narrated by author, Stowe Shockey. I feel fortunate to have met Stowe, who started out with a desire to simply chronicle the life and teachings of one of Franklin, Tennessee's most colorful characters and successful businessmen. She discovered, like I did, the benefit of time spent with Calvin as she received unexpected counseling about her own hopes and dreams—and about challenging life-or-death decisions surrounding her trial with cancer.

I met Stowe and her husband, Peter, through Calvin when I was in Nashville for a seminar about a personal-care products company. I asked Calvin to motivate our local sales force of several thousand people with some success principles and highlights from his life. Afterward, he asked me, as a longtime friend, to take part in an interview. I figured it would be used as a small landmark along the landscape of his journey. Little did I know that those segments would take up two whole chapters. Or, that I would be asked to write the Foreword of this book. It's typical of Calvin, though, to give others a "time to shine."

You're really going to love this insightful book; it will help you identify and replace "limiting" beliefs that hold you back. What you'll find in these pages will give you the courage to not give up through challenging times.

This is your chance to experience, in Calvin's own words, how he made his dreams come true, how he endured through the difficulties of life and along the way, learned to believe in something much bigger than himself. This book germinates the seeds of wisdom—that we are all born with—a divine spark within each of us. I'm grateful that my sons, Michael and Scott (Calvin is their Godfather) and their children, (like you and hopefully your children) can sit down with my old friend Calvin LeHew.

Prepare to be entertained and inspired by his incredible life story as seen through the eyes of a younger dreamer, Stowe Shockey. And may the lessons contained within these pages not only help you face the challenges of life, but serve as encouragement in making your own dreams come true. Don't wait until everything is just right. Things will never be perfect. There will always be challenges, obstacles, and less than ideal conditions. So what? With each step you take, you grow stronger. Always remember, it costs nothing to dream, but everything not to . . .

Love,

Rita Davenport
Author, Speaker, Entrepreneur & TV Host

introduction

Flying high . . . it's the song of birds, music played by wings on the wind, soaring through the skies. For them, flying is as natural as breathing. They were born to it.

For a lot of folks, flying high means freedom from the gravity of fear, a chance to explore the blue vastness of life's possibilities, to look at clouds from the other side, and to see with heightened awareness a panoramic view of God's creation . . .

But for some like me, flying can be a scary proposition. It's sad that a fear of heights keeps some of us from getting airborne, from fulfilling our dreams and our life's purpose. Then again, I guess we're not so much afraid of heights as we are of falling.

But in my dreams I'm not afraid . . . in my dreams I fly. I stand with the sun on my shoulders, spread my wings, and catch the breeze that lifts me toward the crystal heavens—back to the world from where I came—where my spirit longs to be.

Flying high? No, it's not just for birds and the brave. I believe it's what we were all meant to do . . . to ascend toward our God-given gifts. Maybe that's why we're drawn to those who conquer new heights, to those who dare to rise above it all. We want to be like them. We want to fly too . . . like my friend Calvin. It didn't take me long to figure out he is a man who loves to fly.

It also didn't take long to learn that Calvin LeHew is a teacher who spent a lifetime studying the patterns and principles upon which God runs the universe. He is an artistic, out-of-the-box thinker; a perpetual seeker; a pilot of experimental aircraft; and more recently, a cancer survivor. Above all, he's a dreamer who has dared, more than once, to make his dreams come true.

My husband, Peter, and I met Calvin almost two years ago. He had accomplished much in life but he still had one desire—to teach what he knew to be true; from our thoughts and feelings come the words of our mouth. And from the words of our mouth come our lives.

Peter and I shared his vision. Since we are both writers (Peter is also a filmmaker) we decided to create a book and a movie that would encourage others to live out their dreams. We met with Calvin on Monday mornings and from our conversations came the words you now hold in your hands.

While Peter's task was to chronicle my interviews with Calvin on film, mine was to narrate his story in print. In the beginning, I figured Calvin would talk and I would listen. But along the way, I became more than just a listener—I became part of his story. Struggling with life and death decisions surrounding my own cancer—decisions Calvin had also faced earlier that year—I chose to follow his example of overcoming adversity and daring to dream. I found that writing down my feelings and experiences in the spaces between his stories helped me in a most profound way. I was inspired to rise above my fears and to find strength I did not know I had.

This is a story about facing crisis, fulfilling dreams, and a man who taught me how. It began with him telling the story of his life. It ended with changing mine.

No doubt about it . . . he's a man who loves to fly. No, I take that back. Calvin's a man who lives to fly—in every sense of the word. And as I got to know him I imagined that someday, just maybe, I would fly too.

chapter 1

pushing the envelope

Change your thoughts and change your world.

—Norman Vincent Peale

On a cold Tennessee morning in early January 2009, my husband, Peter, and I entered a large brick building known as The Factory. Once a plant used to build stoves during the Depression, the building is now a renovated eclectic shopping center—the brainchild of a man named Calvin LeHew.

I'd met Calvin a few times before but this was my first visit to his office. So far, I knew him to be a leader in the community, a pilot, and a man whose mission in life was "raising consciousness," both in himself and in others. In fact, that's why we were meeting—to discuss doing a book and movie on that topic. Looking back, I realize I was probably in need of having my own consciousness raised. A cancer diagnosis eight months earlier had put me in survival mode and left me feeling low. In a way, it was the perfect starting point for me. There was nowhere to go but up.

We climbed the stairs leading to Calvin's office and knocked on the doorframe. "Come in!" he called. We entered and I immediately noticed the walls, dotted with positive sayings and pictures. Behind Calvin's desk, waist-high shelves housed a number of books. Above, was a large window from the original Stoveworks Factory; 1920s-era windowpanes—twenty-five in all—filled almost the entire wall, providing a glowing backlight for the man who runs The Factory.

In this illuminated state, I got my first glimpse of Calvin in his element. At sixty-nine he looked fit, and very much the same as he did in one of the photos, taken twenty years earlier. He had a full head of hair—just a touch of gray. He was short but stood straight and his silhouette had an upward momentum as though he were outfitted with an invisible rocket backpack and might take off at any minute. No doubt, he'd dreamed of doing that at some point in his life.

He was dressed in an unpretentious blue flight suit, which I learned he wore frequently. Walking around The Factory checking light bulbs and picking up garbage, he was often mistaken for a member of the staff rather than its well-to-do owner.

Seeing us enter the room, he sprang out of his chair with a wide grin and the energy of a man half his age.

"Good-morning! You're looking so goo-ood!" He held out his arms for a hug.

"Good" was pronounced with his distinct Southern accent—two syllables. We laughed and I returned the compliment. This later became our private little joke. As people who faced cancer, we both remembered all too well how friends greeted us during our treatments. You look so good, as we interpreted it, was a polite way of saying, You look pretty good for someone who is dying. Perhaps they didn't mean it that way, but that's the way we heard it.

After setting up his video camera to document our meeting, Peter joined me and we settled back into a pair of antique Queen Anne chairs to listen. Calvin always had a story and this day was no exception.

"I was walking around The Factory as I often do in the mornings, just picking up trash." He began. "I'd already found several pieces of paper when I ran into one of my tenants. As we talked I glanced around looking for a garbage can, but didn't see one. Then I looked at my watch—it was almost time for our meeting so I headed down the hall. I saw a trash can in the coffee shop and I was just about to throw all the paper away when I noticed this envelope."

Calvin held up a weathered envelope. Embossed with tire tracks, it had seen more than a few storms. We noticed the faded handwriting, apparently someone's name. Calvin looked like a kid dying to tell the punch line of a joke.

"Well," his eyes on the envelope, "I studied it for a minute. I wondered, what can this be? Then I turned it over. It was still seee-aled! By then I was thinking there might be something in here."

Peter and I leaned in closer. What treasure had Calvin found? He reached into the envelope, eager to share.

" . . . So I pulled out this check and looked at it. It was from a man who attended a church that rented space here in The Factory. Now, I wasn't wearing my glasses, but it looked like it said one thousand dollars. I was thinking, Wow! Then I looked again. Those zeroes weren't cents. It was a check for one million dollars!"

Peter and I laughed, catching the spirit of the moment. A million dollars! Here was a vivid illustration that Calvin is, indeed, someone who attracts wealth. Who else could go outside, pick up some trash, and find a million dollar check?

"This happened less than an hour ago," he continued. "I haven't called these people yet, so I don't know what the story is. But these things happen . . . these serendipitous moments . . . if your mind is in gear to expect them. They encourage us."

On the wall beside Calvin is a glass showcase with a penny, and, beneath it, a one-dollar bill. Pointing to it, Calvin wasted no time in telling the story behind it.

"I was walking down the street one day on my way to the post office when I saw a penny on the ground, the same one you see right there in the frame. I immediately thought to myself, I can do better than that." He glanced at the picture, then back to me. "So I went into the post office. And I kind of forgot about it—I think that's an important thing to remember—and on my way out, right there in that same spot, was this dollar bill!

"Coincidence?" His eyes narrowed. "Well . . . maybe, but things like that happen all the time to those who believe, with expectancy." Calvin closed his eyes and stretched out his hands, palms up. "When you put a thought in your mind and believe in it and have faith . . . miracles begin to happen."

Quick to make his point, Calvin reached under his desk and pulled out two black leather books. "I have right here in these books many of the little miracles that have happened to me over the years. I keep track of them because it's important to have gratitude." His voice rose in pitch. "I've had so many—two or three a day of these little so-called miracles, serendipities, coincidences—I just had to write them down. You think about someone and they call. Is that a coincidence? You need someone and they show up. Is this an accident? No. Some call it the law of attraction; others call it faith. But I'm convinced it's your intentions that bring these things about. So after you put your desire out there, you just have to have faith, and then . . . "

He paused. "It's like that old saying. Just let go and let God."

⊙ flying high ⊙

more than a coincidence

When the student is ready, the teacher will appear.

—BUDDHIST PROVERB

Calvin intentionally sees the positive in every situation. What others might perceive as nothing more than chance encounters or serendipitous events are, in his view, "little miracles." He even takes time to document these coincidences and give thanks for them.

I like his way of looking at life. I like having faith and believing in miracles too. Maybe that's why I feel my meeting Calvin was more than just chance. I can still hear him say, "You need someone and they show up. Is that an accident?"

I don't think so.

I should tell you how Calvin and I met.

It was December 2007, a blustery day in early winter. Listening to the radio and looking for a street address, I drove down Nashville's legendary Music Row. I was headed to a Christmas party given by one of my old friends Pam Lewis, a successful publicist with her own company, PLA Media. Being back on "The Row" felt strange. My days in the music business were long gone and I was suddenly aware of old wounds that had yet to heal.

I drove slowly, looking from side to side, taking notice of all the changes that had occurred in the last twelve years. *Oh, they renovated that place . . . looks nice.* Finally, I arrived. The parking lot was full. Already I was feeling left out. *Maybe I should go home . . . No, it's just a party.* I took a deep breath and headed inside, reminding myself I wasn't the same scared girl I used to be.

Inside, the air was warm. It smelled of cinnamon, corn chips, and cookies. The music was loud. People were casually dressed—one of my favorite things about Nashville—with a few young men and women who were obvious country music wannabe's. Their hats, tight jeans, and flashy jewelry were dead giveaways. I put my head down and waded through the small crowd. And like everyone who feels out of place at a party, I headed for the food, grabbed some chips and tried to fit in, all the while searching for my friend.

Across the room, I finally spotted Pam. She was talking with someone else so I watched her and waited my turn. Seeing her face took me back in time—it was hard to believe twenty years had blown by since we first met. In those days she was already a hotshot publicist working with several young stars, including Garth Brooks. I was an aspiring young singer and songwriter with a new guitar and a suitcase full of dreams.

I remember the first time we met. Pam came up to my apartment to write a bio on me. I ended up singing for her in my bathroom—it had great acoustics. She never forgot that. Pam is one of the good guys, one who helps those in need. She was good to me, introducing me to producers and publishers who might be interested in my music.

I came to town to be a singer—and I had talent. But, to be honest, I was too full of fear to ever get off the ground. I told myself I was afraid of failing. Looking back, I think I was more afraid of succeeding. *What if things actually went right in my life? That would be too strange.*

In those days, I didn't have a clue that doubting my own gifts was in essence doubting God, who gave those gifts to me . . . that every minute I spent in fear was a moment I had not trusted God. I didn't know my gifts and dreams were so closely tied. All I knew was if you wanted to make it in the music business, you needed a big ego—and I didn't have one.

After being turned down by a few record producers, I decided the life of a songwriter was more to my liking. I consoled myself with the thought that I could still make music and sing, but without all the stress that goes along with being a performer. Make no mistake; the songwriting world is a pressure cooker. Still, I was inspired and went at it hard for five years.

The first few were fun. I got a publishing deal and honed my skills as a writer. All around me people were becoming enormously successful, and I wanted to be like them. So I worked harder. I became highly critical of my work, yet the more I critiqued my music, the further the muse retreated. One day I woke up and realized I was blocked; afraid I couldn't even write a song on my own. It had been a fun ride, but the business of making music had drained me. I'd written with some of the best. I'd met countless music stars. I'd even had a few cuts and one hit single.

Then I quit. I took my pencil and paper, my guitar, and my heartache and quietly left Music Row to start a family.

"Stowe!" Pam stole up behind me. "How are you? Wow, it's been years."

It was good to see her again. We quickly caught up on all the latest. I gave her a few of the books Peter and I had written. She asked about family and if I was singing anywhere. Standard questions. Then she introduced me to a few folks.

"Oh, before you go . . . " Pam grabbed my arm. "What are you doing tomorrow?"

"Uh, nothing I know of . . . "

"Why don't you come out to The Factory? The owner, Calvin LeHew, has this great meeting once a month. It's devoted to raising the awareness of body, mind, and spirit." She waited expectantly for my reply.

"Well," I wasn't sure of what I was getting into. "Okay."

"Great! See you then!"

There are some folks who have a knack for putting people together with one another—Pam is one of those people.

I went to The Factory the next day and enjoyed getting to know a unique group of folks that meet each month to share their own accounts of life—healings and spirituality. I watched as this man named Calvin led the conversation, throwing out ideas and then allowing others to share their stories. Afterward, I introduced myself. "Hi," I shook Calvin's hand. "My name is Stowe . . . like Vermont."

"Stowe . . . " he repeated slowly, making sure he had it right. Up close, the master of ceremonies seemed shy but friendly. "I'm Calvin. It's good to meet you."

We chatted a while. Then I said good-bye and drove home, completely unaware I had just met someone who would play a major role in my life.

chapter 3

the worst day

I will love the light for it shows me the way,
yet I will endure the darkness because it shows me the stars.

—OG MANDINO

It was early February—more than a year since I first met Calvin—and Monday, the day Calvin, Peter and I had agreed for our weekly meetings. Out in the parking lot of The Factory, I stepped from the car. A raindrop hit my cheek. Then another. I glanced up at the darkening clouds and we hurried inside. Moments later, as we settled into Calvin's office, the heavens let loose and we could hear the rains pelting the metal roof.

Today, after several initial interviews, we would begin chronicling his life story—Peter with a camera, me with a laptop. But where to begin? There was a time when Calvin was young and life was often confusing, a time when he was just learning the ropes. There was even a moment early in life when it nearly ended.

Maybe, that would be a good place to start. After all, we're often reminded it's about the journey, not the destination. And since we're not focused on a destination, we have the freedom to do a little time traveling.

So I watch, mesmerized, as the gray in Calvin's sideburns vanishes. Suddenly he has brown hair. And a crew cut. Wrinkles gone! Body toned. I take a breath and relax a little deeper into my chair. Listening intently while the sound of an overhead jet plane shifts down into the low, slow drone of a DC-10's prop engine, I stifle a cough as the smoke of a Viceroy cigarette chokes out the filtered air. From the speakers above, the sultry voice of Nora Jones morphs into the gutsy contralto of Patsy Cline. Finally, the cold of winter fades into the cool breezes of autumn from atop Monteagle, Tennessee.

There I find Calvin, sitting in a vintage World War II-era wooden school desk at Sewanee Military Academy. The year is 1959 and class is in session. Watching his teacher, Calvin leans forward, his chin resting on both hands, when there is a gentle knock on the door.

"Cadet LeHew?"

Calvin immediately straightens at his desk. Sergeant Parker's head pokes inside the classroom door. "Yes, sir?" Calvin answers.

"Colonel Stevens wants to see you." Within moments, Calvin finds himself in the head master's office.

"At ease, Cadet. I just got a call from your father. Your mother is going into the hospital for a minor operation. Nothing to worry about. But . . . if you'd like to take a few days off . . . "

"Yes, sir. I'd appreciate that."

"Alright. Captain Gentry will give you a ride."

"Thank you, sir."

For the first time since he started preparatory school, Calvin is homeward bound, looking forward to seeing the familiar hills of Leipers Fork. He has no way of knowing this will be his last day on the military campus. He hoists his duffle bag over one shoulder and heads out to his commander's car. One look back at the school and he is off.

Soon he is riding shotgun in a '56 Chevy Impala along Tennessee's rough and narrow roads. Always the observer, Calvin notices everything—the tree-covered hills, the fields of corn and tobacco, and the occasional mom and pop gas stations. He also spots a few late-model automobiles with their exciting space-aged-looking fins. Mostly he sees older cars, trucks in particular, and every now and then, a slow-moving tractor.

What he doesn't see are rectangular green destination and exit signs or small shield-shaped blue and red signs with highway numbers. There aren't any semi-trucks rolling on tan pavement either, or scenery blurred by high speeds. This is 1959 and the 46,508-mile web of Interstate Highway System—that will one day play an important part in Calvin's life—is still in its infancy.

They continue north, winding through the mountain roads of the scenic Cumberland Plateau in southeastern Tennessee. A long ride with plenty of time to daydream. Occasionally, Calvin gets a glimpse of his own reflection in the window—his gray uniform, in particular, catches his eye. Later in life, Calvin will strive to keep ego from dominating his thoughts and actions; but young Calvin is full of adolescent pride for who he is becoming. Instinctively, he raises his chin and straightens his tie. His parents will be proud of him. Imagining their faces makes him realize how much he's missed them over the past few months.

At nineteen, Calvin has been away at school for almost a year. He is fulfilling his parent's dream of getting a good education—prep school, solid military training, and then college. With his parent's political connections—they are good friends with Senator Albert Gore and his wife Pauline—there is little doubt he will make it into legendary West Point. "Calvin," his folks often boast, "will be the first LeHew to go to college."

At the halfway mark, Calvin says good-bye to Captain Gentry and climbs into his Uncle Otice's truck. Before long, they arrive at the hospital in Franklin and Calvin gets out, anxious to see his mother. He feels proud, like a soldier returning home from war. Surely his family will notice how he has matured over the last few months. He walks down the hallway and smiles. Then he sees his family.

He stops smiling.

They stand like statues outside the recovery room, stoop-shoul-dered and disoriented. Staring quietly at the floor, his father looks lost. Calvin seeks out the surgeon.

"Son," Doctor Walker says, "you're going to have to be brave." Calvin feels his heart drop to his knees.

"The truth is . . . this was supposed to be a simple procedure on your mother's gallbladder. But . . . " and then he blurts it out: "Calvin, she's full of cancer. I don't think she'll make it more than a few hours." He puts his hand gently on Calvin's shoulder. "Best you can do now is just be with her."

Calvin fights back the tears burning his eyes. The last thing he wants is for his mother to see him cry (fifty years later, he still holds back those tears). In the recovery room she is semi-conscious. Calvin pulls up a chair, leans into the bed and takes her hand. He finds it hard to speak. *What do you say when the only woman you've ever loved is about to die?*

"Calvin . . . " She whispers through labored breathing. "You look . . . so . . . handsome."

He swallows hard. It feels as if there is a pit in his throat. "Mom . . . " He can't even finish his sentence so he does all he knows how to do—he squeezes her hand gently every so often and, in return, she squeezes his back. But as the moments tick by, he feels her grip slipping away. Within a few hours, she is gone.

Under ever-changing clouds, the family gathers at the cemetery plot. After a few words from Reverend Galloway, and rituals unforeseen days earlier, the coffin is lowered into the raw earth. They stand, silent, lost in their own reflections.

The last three days are a hazy collage of funeral arrangements, telephones ringing, flowers, bundt cakes, and the shuffling in-and-out of family and friends. Calvin can hardly believe his mother is truly gone. He is trapped in a horrible nightmare and there is no one to comfort him.

The LeHews pride themselves on being a strong family. Displays of affection are rare. All his young life, Calvin has been reminded: "LeHews don't cry."

Around the house, family members struggle quietly with their loss. Calvin stares out the front window when his sister approaches him. "Calvin . . . " She casts her eyes at the floor, then back at her brother. "I don't know how to tell you this . . . but Daddy's sick."

His right shoulder flinches. "What kind of sick?" he continues staring into the distance.

"Calvin, look at me." His jaw firmly clenched, he faces her. "He's got cancer too," her voice is shaking. "And the doctor says he doesn't have long . . . maybe just a few months."

One day a budding student in a prestigious military academy, the next a soldier in the trenches of life. Now every moment is surreal. Taking shallow breaths and stuffing his pain deep within, Calvin lives on instinct. Occasionally, he allows himself to wonder what his classmates back at school might be doing. For once, homework and tests don't seem like such a chore. What he wouldn't give to be back within the safety of Sewanee Academy.

He can hardly believe mere weeks have passed since that fateful day he lost his mother. And now his father . . .

When his dad pleads, "Don't let me die in the hospital," Calvin and his two sisters, Jane and Barbara, dutifully honor his wishes. Long days merge into even longer nights. There is an endless routine of feeding and cleaning. There are the shots—morphine, for his pain. Calvin and his sister take turns administering them. Bedridden and broken-hearted, his father calls out for their mother in the middle of the night. Mired in a slow, painful death, Calvin's father wants to get on with it.

"Calvin," he pleads, "kill me . . . take me out of my misery. Please, son . . . " His breath is shallow. "I'm in *pain* . . . "

"You know I can't do that, Dad."

"Then give me a butcher knife. I'll do it myself."

Morphine is the only way Calvin knows to comfort him, but even the higher doses do little to ease his father's pain so the butcher knife conversations continue . . . it's almost more than Calvin can bear.

Three months after his mother—his father dies.

How does a teenager confront the death of . . . not just one, but both parents? Trying not to think about it is one option. You try to forget that your parents will never know you as an adult; that they'll never see your wedding, or your children. There'll be no one to guide you in making important decisions. There'll be no more chances to hear them say, "I love you . . . " Who do you turn to on the worst day of your life? On any other day Calvin would take comfort in his dog, Shep. But Shep has been missing for the last week and Calvin had spent hours walking the hillsides calling for him.

On the way home from his father's funeral, Calvin sees something moving in the tall grass beside their driveway. His heart leaps at the sight of his long lost dog. He has finally come home.

"Shep!" Calvin runs to greet him. But it isn't the happy reunion he imagined. Up close, he sees Shep is horribly wounded, dragging himself onto the gravel drive by his front paws. Calvin drops to his knees and cradles Shep's head in his hands. He glances at his backside and the sight almost makes him vomit—Shep is covered in maggots. A wave of hopelessness chokes Calvin and he looks up into the skies. *Oh, God. Not this . . . not Shep too.*

There is no veterinarian to turn to. No one to call—and as far as Calvin can see—no other choice but to put Shep out of his misery. He walks to the house to fetch his Winchester rifle, the same gun he used to go hunting with Shep. Moments later he points the barrel between his dog's beautiful brown eyes, then closes his own—"G'bye, boy. . . "—and squeezes the trigger.

Calvin digs a grave out by the edge of the yard and buries his last best friend. His world, as he knows it, has come to an end. Everyone has left him, so it seems. All alone, dark clouds of despair cover any ray of hope that may have lingered in his heart. There is only one thing left to do . . .

He takes a shower and combs his hair. Not one who usually wears pajamas, this evening he finds some and puts them on. Next, he goes to the medicine cabinet and searches for some kind of poison. He finds a large bottle of aspirin. *This should do it.* He takes the whole bottle. Then, he lies down on his bed and crosses his arms over his chest. Hoping to see his parents and Shep again, Calvin is ready to die.

Floating peacefully backward through the bright window of Calvin's office, I found myself staring at him from across the desk, his image blurred by my own tears. I took a slow, deep breath. I had no idea what to say. How could so much tragedy strike someone so young, in such a short period of time?

"So . . . what happened?" I finally asked.

"Well, I awoke to this incredibly beautiful day . . . the morning light just filled my room. And somehow life seemed to get better after that. Maybe it was that beautiful sun shining down on me in bed . . . or maybe it was because I realized I'd already gone through the valley of death, and life could never be that bad again. It was truly the beginning of a new day, for me."

I shook my head, amazed that a young man could have such a deep revelation.

"But you know the thing I remember most?" He clasped his hands and held them to his chest.

"No," I waited for some great pearl of wisdom. "What?"

"Waking up that morning with a splitting headache . . . and not a single aspirin in the house!"

blog therapy

We teach best what we most need to learn.

—Richard Bach

C alvin's worst day reminds me of similar times in my own life. We all have them—those days, weeks, or sometimes years when life seems to sneak up and strike with ferocious strength. Where and when and how it happens shapes us . . . sometimes for the good. Sometimes not.

As I get to know Calvin, I learn that he and I have a few things in common. Trauma early in life . . . cancer later. *Is there a correlation?* I also recognize in him something I see in my own mirror—a certain numbness to the pain we endured as young people. Our tears have been few.

I wonder, in our attempt to be strong, if we've given enough sympathy for our inner child? I know in my own life, I've often downplayed, even laughed at, some of the tragedies I've experienced; like the death of my mother when I was three, the struggles with my alcoholic father, the abuse I received in foster homes, and the difficulties I had with my deaf brother. So many years trying to hold it in . . . when the child inside was longing to let it out.

Some people believe holding onto grief is literally toxic. It could be. Still, I wonder, *can pain actually manifest itself in the form of a disease?* I don't know.

I do see how restraining our grief can affect us negatively, especially as adults. Holding back the tears is like plugging up a bathtub and turning on the spigot—before long we are drowning in our sorrow. Not only does it depress us, it affects our health, our careers, and the lives of those around us.

In one of my previous books, *Journey of Light*, I learned the value of journaling about past memories. The simple act of writing about my childhood, digging up those buried emotions, was extremely therapeutic. I'll never forget the tears I cried as I wrote—how sweet they were. Putting my thoughts on paper healed me.

In today's Internet world, the term *blog* is used to refer to a web-log—a journal or diary of one's thoughts, experiences, rants and reflections. For this book, I'd like to call that device what it really is: *Blog Therapy*. In it, I can bend time, give mature thoughts to my inner child, and speak wisdom to my past and future self. I usually just start writing, trying to find my voice from a time of life that was troublesome. There is a certain fear whenever I begin—that something awful will be uncovered—that I will descend into deep depression. That has never happened. Facing grief is frightening, but not as frightening as the consequences of holding onto it. Journaling, or blogging, is an opportunity to shed a few tears, then move on with life.

In that spirit, I write my first entry in this book. Something about Calvin's story opens a window into my past; giving me a glimpse of the little girl I was and, on some level, still am. If I had kept a journal or blog when I was three years old, it might have gone something like this:

August 1964
Daddy and me are leaving the big hospital building where mommy stays

now. She doesn't live with us anymore. Daddy is very quiet. He holds my hand tight going down the long stairs to the lobby—our footsteps sound sad as they echo off the pretty blue tiled walls. Mommy was sleepy today but maybe we can come back again tomorrow. Maybe she'll be awake. There's not much to do in mommy's room . . . her bed is very high . . . but I like the smell of the cool air that comes out of the big box under her window . . . It feels good. Before we left, Daddy picked me up so I could wave bye-bye to mommy. I don't think she feels good.

Writing down memories from my childhood point-of-view feels surprisingly good. Cathartic. As I reread the words from this imaginary diary, I feel somehow more connected to Calvin's life story . . . his journey is getting into my head and heart in unexpected ways. Journaling my own reactions to his story seems to make it easier for me to connect emotionally to the book we're writing. Maybe it will even help me. I make another entry from this same time frame.

September 1964

"Daddy . . . Where's mommy?"

He tilts his head a little and looks at me with a sad expression. Then, reaching down, he picks me up and sets my tiny, three-year-old body on his lap. "Your mother," his voice sounds high and shaky, "has . . . gone to heaven . . . " He takes a deep breath, then lets it out. "She died."

I sit quietly on his lap and stare at the floor. "Can I go outside and play now?"

"Yes, go ahead."

The next day I try again. "Daddy, where is mommy?"

an elevated perspective

We are not human beings having a spiritual experience.
We are spiritual beings having a human experience.

—Pierre Teilhard De Chardin

Calvin and I had been chatting for about twenty minutes when one of his employees interrupted us. He rose from his desk. "Will you excuse me a minute?"

While I waited, I scanned the room. Everywhere I looked, I noticed aviation symbols and pictures of airplanes on the wall. Over in the corner, model planes hung from the ceiling. And on Calvin's desk was a row of small replicas of old aircraft, mostly gifts from admirers. Calvin's clock was even an airplane with the propeller for hands.

I inhaled deeply and stared out the wavy panes of glass. Using my imagination, I left reality for a moment, drawn through the melted sands that separate us from the outside world. I was fantasizing about floating out and flying through the beautiful deep blue of the January sky when Calvin returned to his desk.

Without thinking I asked, "Calvin, what's it's like when you're flying up there . . . you know, all alone?"

He smiled. "It's what I live for." And just like that, his eyes took on a faraway look. "There's something about being up high. Being elevated. It helps me see the big picture. And I guess I like . . . living on the edge. Testing things. It's scary, but the reward is worth it—reminds me of taking out a big loan . . . risky. There's always the possibility I might crash."

I was suddenly sobered. "Have you ever crashed?"

"Oh, yeah . . . " he held up his right hand, fingers spread wide. "Five times. My wife says I got brain damage on the first one."

I laughed nervously. "Sounds like it."

"There are so many things that can go wrong. You can run out of gas or daylight. Your compass can go haywire and suddenly you're in unfamiliar territory. Some just give up and crash, but you learn that you can land and come out ok."

I squirmed in my seat. Although I thought of myself as someone who was not afraid to *die*, listening to Calvin made me realize one thing—I was afraid to crash. Funny, he seemed at peace with the idea.

"So . . . you're not afraid of dying?"

"Nope," he said with confidence. "I've lived a good life and when it's my time, I'll go. Hopefully it'll be while I'm flying."

Though he appeared peaceful, I couldn't help wondering. "Were you ever afraid of dying?"

"Yeah . . . " He said after a thoughtful pause. "When I was a little kid. But after my folks passed away, all that changed. Once you've lived through the worst day of your life . . . and you've looked at death from both sides of the mirror, well . . . you get a different perspective on living . . . And it doesn't hurt to have a few plane crashes under your belt."

I groaned and looked at him like he was crazy. He grinned from ear to ear, obviously amused by my fidgety reaction.

"The last plane crash I had—and I do hope it's the last—changed my life tremendously. I actually had a near-death experience."

"Really?" I knew something about near death experiences from the docudrama Peter made, *Life After Life*. I was all ears. "What happened?"

"I was taking off in my gyrocopter . . . "

"A gyrocopter?"

"It's basically a one-man helicopter but it also has an engine-pow-ered propeller to provide thrust. A helicopter lifts you up into the air, but a gyrocopter needs a longer runway and cooler, denser air for take off. It was a hot July day . . . that was my first mistake. I was taking off in a small field—that was my second one. I realized right away I wasn't going to make it over the trees. I had two choices—either hit the trees or put the gyrocopter into the ground. By habit, I pushed the stick down and headed toward earth, tumbling through the air. I crashed.

"It was in that moment, at that instant, that I became conscious that I was *above* the crash. My awareness suddenly lifted and I could see everything. There was total silence, stillness, and peace. No fear whatsoever. Over in the garden I could see my wife, Marilyn, working. Hearing the crash, she immediately called 911.

"Soon, paramedics from the local hospital arrived and I became conscious . . . coming back to my body. A man hovered over me with a worried expression. 'Mr. Lehew, you're too far gone. You'll never make it to the Williamson County Hospital. We're going to have to life flight you to Vanderbilt Hospital.'

"Funny, I didn't feel that bad off . . . but since I like helicopters, I figured this was a good excuse to get to ride in one. This is where my past programming started working for me. I began seeing the positive in everything. Instead of getting stressed and fearful, I just let go and enjoyed the experience, like an observer.

"I remember the helicopter coming in—I helped them steer clear of the TVA power lines. And then my wife, Marilyn, was standing beside me saying, 'Calvin, you won't believe how good looking these nurses are!'"

I laughed. "Marilyn . . . she's an understanding woman."

Calvin closed his eyes and nodded. "Yes, she is, Stowe, and she was right, too! Even though I was in a neck brace and could only see above me, when those nurses bent down to help lift me onto the gurney, well . . . I couldn't help but notice how attractive they were, especially in their zipper-front, blue jumpsuits. They put me on the helicopter, gave me a morphine shot, and then these women began taking off my clothes! By the time we lifted off, I thought *I had died and gone to Heaven.*

"During the flight to the hospital, I had a little flashback. Back when my father was dying, I applied to Vanderbilt University. He really wanted me to go to college and, of course, I wanted to make his dreams come true. But on his deathbed I recall him saying 'Son, with your grades, you'll never make it into Vanderbilt.' Turned out he was right. But lying on that stretcher that day, I thought, *I'm finally getting admitted to Vanderbilt.*

"Soon, we landed on the heliport atop Vanderbilt Hospital. As they wheeled me in, a nurse from the hospital came up to me. 'Calvin, what are you doing here?' Then, from another direction, 'Is that Calvin LeHew?' For a moment I thought maybe I *had* died and gone to heaven . . . or somewhere. Next I saw the father of the local Episcopal Church, Bob Cowperthwaite. I reached out to him. 'Father, Are you here to give me last rites?'

"'No,' he said, 'I just happened to be in the neighborhood and I heard you were here.' The nurse who had spoken to me turned out to be a woman I knew from Franklin.

"It was just another time where I was reminded, you don't have to take the negative view. That out-of-body experience gave me an elevated perspective on life and death. I really believe that *with every adversity there lies within it a seed of greatness.*"

"I like that saying."

"Me too. I was young when I first heard that . . . it shaped my outlook on life."

"Like seeing the glass half full?"

"Yep," He grinned, "it's all in how you look at it."

january 26, 2009

*T*HE DAY IS *almost over. As I stare out at the dark grey sky I am reminded of winters past, and how I came to look at life as a young person. They are random memories, falling gently like snowflakes against the window of my soul, memories about one of my deepest life-long fears: Cancer.*

Rewind to winter, 1977. I am a teenager. I hang out with my father during the evening in the warmth of our kitchen. While I take cooking lessons from him, he drinks wine and spouts off fun facts about history, movies, and life in general. Occasionally it turns serious.

"Now, Stowe," he waves both hands for emphasis, "you need to remember to do monthly breast self-examinations—"

"Aww, Dad . . . please."

"No, no, I'm serious. Don't forget—your grandmother died of uterine cancer at 54 and your mother died of breast cancer at 34—"

"I know, I know. It gets younger every generation . . . " I roll my eyes. "Since I'm sixteen, shouldn't I be dead already?"

Such are the conversations and memories that shape my thinking about this terrible illness and my chances of getting it. Still, I never really feel like I will have breast cancer. In fact, I am even somewhat cavalier about it, only doing self-exams occasionally.

Fast forward ten years. I am settling into bed one night when I scratch under my arm and feel something. A lump. I am twenty-six and new to Nashville, Tennessee—here to make my mark in the music business—and suddenly all I can think about are my father's haunting words. I am paralyzed with fear.

A week later I have a biopsy. The lump is benign. I've made it through. Although I still believe I am above breast cancer, I allow the thoughts of a premature death to creep into my consciousness.

A few more years go by, and I pass the age of my mother's death at age thirty-four. It feels like a milestone—I've lived beyond her. Still, somewhere inside, I hear the clock ticking . . . ticking.

My grandfather, grandmother, and mother all died of cancer. Three of my cousins survived it. One day, when I am thirty-nine, my father calls.

"Stowe," he rasps into the phone. "The doctor says I have lung cancer."

Nine months later he is gone.

I decide to discard his prior words of doom. I do my best to take care of my body, eating nutritious foods and exercising regularly. If being healthy can outsmart a disease, I will be the healthiest person I know. But there is more to living than just being physically healthy. I walk in darkness, unaware of what I'm doing. Instead of focusing on living in the present moment, I am obsessed with trying to outsmart death. I live—as many people do—in a state of denial. Everyone knows they're going to die, but nobody believes it.

One day our youngest daughter, Grace snuggles against me. "Mommy, when I grow up, can we live near each other?"

"Of course we can, sweetie." I hug her and give her a confident smile. Then, I stare out the window at a withering dogwood tree in the front yard . . . wondering what the future will hold.

———— ⧓ ————

who's who

For weeks, Calvin promised to give me a private tour of The Factory. Today was the day. So far, I'd only seen a few stores and I looked forward to getting the inside scoop on how Calvin's vision became a reality. I knocked on his door. No answer. I glanced at my watch—9:00—I was on time. So I knocked again, this time poking my head inside the door. "Good-morning." I surveyed the empty room. "Calvin?"

"I'm in here . . . " came a muffled voice, "in the conference room."

Entering the adjacent room, I saw Calvin standing behind a large antique table. He put down the big box he was holding, then came around and gave me a hug. Stepping back I noticed the neat piles of letters and photos on the table. "What are you doing?"

"Oh, just going through some memorabilia."

I glanced around at the stacks of framed pictures and news clippings—there were hundreds. "Where'd all these come from?""

"My past." Calvin swept his hand over the collection. "I call them my 'ego awards.'"

"*Ego* awards?"

"Yes. I got most of them years ago. Having souvenirs like this used to make me feel fulfilled, you know, hobnobbing with famous people, getting their autographs, things like that. It used to boost my self-image, but now . . . now it just feels like braggadocio."

I flipped through some of the framed photos leaning against the wall, photos of Calvin with a virtual "Who's Who" of celebrities. Singers, politicians, scientists, astronauts, you name it. I was especially drawn to the pictures of familiar country music singers, ones I had also met.

Calvin looked over my shoulder. "Those are some of the Nashville stars who've done concerts here at The Factory. We've had Martina McBride, Lorrie Morgan, Vince Gill, Faith Hill, Kenny Chesney, Reba McEntire . . . there've been quite a few."

Next to Reba's picture was a photo of Calvin standing with one of Nashville's most famous icons. "You knew Minnie Pearl?"

"Yes, we were friends. We worked together for the American Cancer Society." Calvin moved back and pointed to some other familiar faces. "Here are the Judds . . . there's Marilyn and me with Wynonna, Naomi, and Ashley. They're great people."

Over to the side were some posters. "Lyle Lovett . . . Bonnie Raitt and . . . and Michael McDonald?"

"Yes, they've all played here."

Moving to the other side of the room, I saw an official-looking photo of Calvin and Al Gore. "Is this at the White House?"

"Yes, ma'am." He pointed to another photo of himself with Al. "That's us at the Natchez Trace Parkway dedication ceremony. I had to give a speech, so I told how I used to babysit him when I was a teenager in Washington, D.C.— "

"You *babysat* Al Gore?"

"Yes, I did. I told the audience, 'You see those Secret Service agents behind us, and those pins they're wearing? I should probably be wearing one because I was actually Al's first bodyguard.' Well, Al waved over one of the guards and actually took the secret service pin off his lapel, came over . . . and," Calvin pointed to the jacket he was wearing in the picture, "he pinned it on me!"

I grinned. "Calvin LeHew—Bodyguard to the vice-president . . . "

We continued down a short hall leading to the entryway and I saw a picture of someone I used to hang out with years ago—Garth Brooks. "How do you know Garth?"

"Back in the late nineties, John Kennedy, Jr. asked Garth for an interview for *George* magazine. John offered to meet him anywhere in the United States.' Garth said, 'Well, there's this place called The Factory . . .'"

"So they met here?"

"Yes. Garth made the cover of *George* magazine. Let's see, they were here on . . ." Calvin squinted at the date on the photo, "February 11, 1999—not long before John-John was killed in the plane crash."

We walked in silence to another area of pictures. There was one of an older pilot standing in front of a stealth fighter plane. "Who's this?"

"That's Chuck Yeager, one of my heroes. I like him because he's such a risk taker. I actually got this picture because of Naomi Judd. She and President Bush, Sr. were down in Florida with Chuck when Naomi mentioned to them about her friend, Calvin, who'd lived through five plane crashes." Calvin laughed. "I'm sure *that* impressed Chuck Yeager! Next thing I know, Chuck sends me this photo of himself. He signed it, 'To Calvin LeHew, Fly Safe, Chuck Yeager.'"

I pointed to a photo of a young guy in a flight suit. "Who's this pilot?"

"That's me, back in 1962, climbing into a T-33 jet at Reese Air Force Base in Lubbock, Texas. I was in the Air Force ROTC during college, and then joined the Tennessee Air National Guard during the Vietnam era."

Next, Calvin waved his hand in the direction of a picture and a handwritten letter. "That's from Norman Vincent Peale. I admired his

28   ∞ flying high ∞

work greatly. So one day I wrote him a check, but just for fun decided not to sign it." Calvin chuckled. "I enclosed a note saying, *I will sign this when I see you at the speaker's conference in Atlanta.* Peale was the main speaker, and just before he went on I jumped on the stage and stuck out my hand, 'Dr. Peale, I'm Calvin LeHew and— '

"'Calvin!' He jumped up and reached in his pocket, 'I have something here for you to sign!' I laughed and said, 'You preachers are all the same—you like money!' We both had a nice laugh."

To the right of Dr. Peale's photo was a plaque: *Imagineering at The Factory* . . .

"Yes, Disneyworld used that word, *Imagineering*, in some of their promotions. I liked it. Albert Einstein said something, which I added below it, 'Imagination is more important than knowledge.'" Calvin paused, "That reminds me of a bumper sticker I saw the other day; 'Worry is the WRONG use of IMAGINATION.'"

"Ah . . . good one," I said, turning my attention back to the remaining pictures in the room. Most were on the floor. "Seems like you've got a lot of valuable memories here. What are you going to do with them?"

Calvin shrugged. "I don't know, Stowe. I'll probably put them in storage. They don't mean that much to me anymore."

We stood quietly for a moment. It was amazing how much memorabilia one man could collect in a lifetime.

"Oh, here's something else . . . " Calvin moved toward his desk. "Just some inspirational things I tore out of books." He picked up a few pages with ragged edges. "Here are the Beatitudes . . . If I'm ever feeling down, I read them and they change my consciousness. And here's a quote I like:

> *"Keep your thoughts positive, because your thoughts*
> *become your words.*
> *Keep your words positive, because your words*
> *become your behaviors.*

Keep your behaviors positive, because your behaviors
become your habits.
Keep your habits positive, because your habits
become your values.
Keep you values positive, because your values
become your destiny. "
—GANDHI

Calvin stopped, then tapped two fingers on the desk. "Okay. Are you ready to tour The Factory?"

I nodded and held out my hand toward the door. "Show me the way."

factory tour

Imagination always wins out over willpower. Always. Learn to see THROUGH your eyes, not WITH your eyes. Be a visionary, a dreamer, and engineer your life with 'Imagineering.'

—FROM CALVIN'S *MANIFESTING DREAMS*

As we stepped into the entrance, I noticed right away a painted sign, made to look like white chalk on a school blackboard. *Things are ideas in Form.— by Ernest Holmes*

"That sure describes The Factory." I said.

"Yes. This place is nothing more than an idea brought to form by action. I've put signs like these all around the place. They mean something to me . . . I hope they mean something to others."

Across the hall, I saw another one. *Shoot for the Moon. Even if you miss you'll land among the stars.—Brian Littrell*

It struck me how Calvin used these positive messages in his unique shopping mall—a sharp contrast to the subliminal Madison Avenue messages in most malls.

Near the front lobby, Calvin pointed to some old kitchen stoves on display. "These are the three types of stoves that were manufactured here: Allen started the place in 1929, then a few years later there was Dortch Stove Works, and then Magic Chef from 1955-59. I was just a kid when many of my family and friends worked here. Jamison Bedding took over the building for a time, but after they left it sat vacant for years. Eventually, the city of Franklin, which by then owned it, wanted to get rid of it."

"And that's where you came in . . . "

"Yes." Calvin pointed to another one of the blackboard signs. *Missing the mark is one of the ways in which we learn to hit the target. Failure is a vital part of achieving success.—Eric Butterworth.*

We walked a little farther. "And here's another. *Obstacles, when viewed from a higher point of view are invariably stones on the pathway to success—Dr. Raymond Holliwell.* That's probably one of the reasons I like flying—it gives me that different perspective."

We entered the commons area, and off to the right, I saw a beautiful open-aired restaurant. "This is *Stoveworks*," Calvin said. "My wife, Marilyn, started this restaurant to bring ladies and, of course, their men, into The Factory.

"Over there is Jamison Hall, the second largest meeting room in The Factory . . . looks like there's a seminar going on right now."

We proceeded down the main hallway, passing art galleries, boutiques, craft shops, and other unique stores. Calvin held his arm out, "Every business here is either artistic, creative, unique, musical, or to do with food. There's no K-Mart, Wal-Mart, Sears, or Dillards—no big chain stores. They are mostly run by women that have never been in business before—very creative, right-brained kind of people." Calvin pointed to the second floor balcony, "Even our offices upstairs reflect that kind of thinking."

"So, you're giving others a chance to parlay their imagination into success?"

He nodded. "We have eleven learning centers here at The Factory. They teach everything from art, drama, vocals, and musical instruments to film, fashion design, cooking, and dance."

We continued down the hall. "So what are some of the lessons you've learned from this whole Factory experience?"

"Well, you've got to have an open mind. This place didn't just happen. We worked at these kinds of things for years." He pointed to a string of individual art shops, "We call this area 'The Row.' I got the idea from The Torpedo Factory near Washington, D.C., and I thought it would be unique around here, something different."

Everywhere I looked, I noticed the marriage of old and new; weathered barn board and contemporary stairways; aged concrete with modern designs painted over it; an antique store next to a fashionable salon."

"It looks so organic . . . "

"And up there." Calvin pointed to the ceiling. "See those hanging assembly lines? They go throughout the whole Factory. That's where the stoves used to hang while being assembled. They add character . . . And look!" Calvin knelt to pet a customer's dog. "Dogs are permitted here. After all, they're only human . . . " he grinned.

Anyone who knows Calvin knows how much he loves animals. *Happy Tales Humane* for pet adoptions is one of The Factory's busiest stores, and one of Calvin's favorite charities.

Farther down the corridor, we came upon an auditorium. The sign overhead read, *Liberty Hall*. "This is The Factory's largest concert venue, which seats about 2,000. CMT—Country Music Television—regularly films music concerts here."

Over to the side, I read another chalkboard sign. *Our achievements today are but the sum of our thoughts of yesterday— Pascal.*

"I think that's powerful," Calvin said. "And over here is a sign . . . I asked permission from the churches that rent space here before I put it up. It says, *Anyone who will search for the science in religion and the religion in science will find they harmonize and prove each other—Charles Fillmore.* I think we'll see how that plays out in the future as science and religion come closer together."

"I love how you put these quotes everywhere. It reflects your vision of the place."

Calvin put his hands in his pockets. "I just wanted to share them with those who are open to the message . . . some folks come and hunt for them, like it's a game.

The long hallway was filled with people—young, old, and in-between—walking together, shopping, talking, laughing, or just having a quiet moment. Calvin had definitely designed a positive space, a place that drew people together, his own personal creation—sort of like a song is for me. I could see Calvin was pleased to share it with others.

"Marilyn and I have a desire to give back to the community. Doing things from the heart—that's important . . . and where we find true happiness. It's what's needed in the world. More giving, more loving. For me, it's helping animals and disadvantaged children . . . and teaching. The Factory is a learning center. I want to help people look outside their blockages, beyond their limitations, to encourage them to see the possibilities and to have hope, even in the face of adversity or crisis."

Every area of trouble gives out a ray of hope;
and the one unchangeable certainty is that
nothing is certain or unchangeable
—JOHN FITZGERALD KENNEDY

february 9, 2009

*H*OW DOES SOMEONE *find hope in the face of a crisis? I've wondered that more than a few times over the last ten months. At the first sign that something was wrong—I hoped it would go away. When I searched online, Googling my symptoms—rectal bleeding—I hoped for a simple diagnosis, something like hemorrhoids. But on the day I finally went to the doctor—when the world as I knew it came crashing down around me—I hoped for only one thing; to make it through that first dark night.*

It was April 15, 2008, the anniversary of the night my husband, Peter, and I met. We loved remembering that evening from nineteen years earlier; a blind date, a movie called The Dream Team, and the two of us talking and laughing in the darkened theater . . . getting to know one another. Before long we were coming up with our own dreams and ideas of things to do together. Somewhere along the way we took to calling ourselves 'The Dream Team,' a name that lives on today.

We usually go out for dinner to celebrate this special anniversary but on this day we're doing something different, something not quite so romantic. This day, I'm having a colonoscopy. I've been bleeding for a few months and now it's time to see what's going on.

"Right this way, Mrs. Shockey," the nurse holds out her hand to lead the way.

I take my first step out of the small dressing room. There are people—patients and their spouses—everywhere. I'm self-conscious, clutching the skimpy hospital gown around my naked frame. Can't someone design something to wear in the hospital that doesn't have gaping holes in it? I walk past the serious faces. The floor is cold and I'm trembling.

"Ok, Mrs. Shockey. If you'll just lie down here . . . " I make myself halfway comfortable. Then the nurse carefully inserts an IV-needle into my arm and explains that during the examination they'll administer Demerol as a painkiller and Versed as a tranquilizer in order to make me drowsy and relaxed for the exam. "Now just take it easy," she says. "The doctor will be here shortly."

I glance around at the strange tools of the gastro-intestinal doctor. He has two television monitors—I wonder, Is one for him and one for me? There are a lot of fancy computer gadgets. Then I look behind me. That's when I see it—the long, flexible tube with the miniature wide-angle lens on the end, the single most feared object in the room—the dreaded colonoscope. It's about the width of an index finger but the length seems staggering. Maybe I should think about something else.

Outside, it's a beautiful sunny morning. But there's not much happening in the parking lot, so I turn my attention to the music coming from the ceiling speakers. An old Elton John song catches my ear and I close my eyes. "Don't let the sun go down on me . . . "

Someone speaks behind me. "Good morning, Stowe." I'm Doctor James. You ready to get started?"

"Uh, yes . . . but I was wondering, is it possible for me to stay awake for the procedure? I want to watch it."

"Well, we'll try and keep the tranquilizer dosage low, but it's hard to

say how your body will respond. Some people are able to stay awake, but most don't remember anything. We'll just have to see."

Suddenly, a wave of sleepiness washes over me. It is all I can do to keep my eyes open. C'mon, Stowe . . . you . . . can do it. I sense the doctor behind me. In front of me, I see the blurry images of my insides. Though I don't feel any pain, there is definitely something going on "down there." The doctor's occasional comments sound dreamlike and far away.

"There's a polyp . . . ok, got it."

I try to focus. His voice fades in and out. "Hm, I don't like the looks of that . . . "

Everything is surreal. Then, darkness.

A nurse rubs my shoulder. "Mrs. Shockey?"

"Hm?" I struggle to open my eyes.

"It's all over now, sweetie. I'm going to wheel you into recovery. I'll have your husband come help you."

Surrounded now by blue hospital curtains and the voices of strangers on either side of me, I sit up in bed, confused. My head is swimming. I reach out in slow motion for my clothes and begin dressing. Peter sticks his head through the curtains, appearing to me like the sun through dark, grey clouds. I'm glad to see him.

"How's my girl?" he smiles at me.

"Ok," I slowly get to my feet.

"How did it go?" He takes me in his arms. "Did he say anything?"

Suddenly I feel weak. It's all coming back to me now. "Uhm . . . he said . . . he said I have cancer."

It's been almost a year since I got that news and not a day goes by that I don't live with the reality of those words: I have cancer.

goals to dream by

One ship sails East
And another West,
By the self-same winds that blow,

Tis the set of the sails
And not the gales,
That tells the way we go.

—ELLA WHEELER WILCOX

The morning sounds of The Factory were everywhere. Outside, trucks making deliveries. Downstairs, large garage doors rumbling open and slamming shut. And out in the hallway, office workers planning their day. Inside Calvin's office, I settled back into my chair, pulled out my laptop and pressed the "start" button. Over the last few months I'd gotten in the habit of recording our conversations and then transcribing them at home.

"Calvin, I've heard that you counsel people sometimes . . . kind of help them get their businesses going. Is that a consultation service you charge for?"

"No, no, absolutely not. That's just my way of giving back. I believe in helping others. 'To whom much is given, much is expected.' That's one of the principles I live by."

"Where did you get all these principles? You didn't come from a wealthy, or particularly well-educated, family . . . "

"No," he laughed softly. "I was born above my father's little country store. He had a third-grade education. My mom went as far as the sixth grade. And I went to school in a two-room schoolhouse that didn't even have indoor plumbing. So, no, we weren't wealthy by any stretch of the imagination . . . not poor, either. But, I was *raised* around a lot of poverty consciousness."

"So how'd you learn to rise above it?"

"My father had a sawmill and a small store, so he knew a lot of folks. One of his friends was Albert Gore, senior . . . before he became a senator. In fact, Dad helped him get elected. I guess it was because of their friendship that I had the opportunity to become a page in the United States Senate. Now, you talk about a country boy growing up fast in the big city! It was the first time I'd worn a coat and tie. And the first time I'd been in an air-conditioned building.

"I started as a Senate page back in 1956. I did it for a while before coming back to Tennessee. After my folks died, the Gores took me under their wing, and I went to school in Washington, D.C., and worked as an elevator operator in the Senate office building. Mrs. Gore—Pauline—was strict. She made sure I kept up with my studies.

"I loved Washington and I learned a lot there. I guess it was while working on Capitol Hill that I first saw what I thought of as *greatness*. Maybe it was all in my mind, but the people I met seemed to me . . . bigger than life. I mean, here I was a kid from Leipers Fork, running errands on a daily basis for Lyndon B. Johnson, Richard Nixon, and John Kennedy. I was actually getting to know them personally. I got to know five presidents while I worked there. I studied them . . . and what made them successful.

"Of course, being so young, I was impressed by the glamour of it all . . . " Calvin folded his arms across his chest. "Back then I thought success meant having money. I wanted to be rich like them. But after my parents died, I felt obligated to go to college. That was all they'd ever wanted for me. So even though I didn't know what I wanted to do, I went to college. I was in my junior year at George Washington University with no thoughts of leaving D.C., when Mrs. Gore came up to me one day in the halls of Congress . . . Now, please understand, she was a strong woman and I respected her. When she talked, I listened. That day she looked me dead in the eye and asked me, 'Calvin, what are you going to do with your life?' I just stood there. I knew I had to think fast.

"'Well,' I said, 'I guess . . . I'm going to be a congressman.'

"'Ok,' Mrs. Gore nodded, as if the deal was sealed. 'Then, you'll have to go back to your home state and go to the University of Tennessee and graduate.'

"So I did. It wasn't long, though, before I realized I didn't really want to be a congressman. I liked my freedom too much. But I continued on with my studies and took a lot of great courses, including business and my two favorites—psychology and philosophy. Funny, but they came about as kind of an accident . . . just electives I took on a whim because they fit in with my schedule. But once I got into them, I thought, *Hey, this stuff really makes sense.* I was so interested in all of it. I'd say it had a real bearing on my life.

"It was around this time, Stowe, that I first heard about these principles I based my life on. It started one night when my fraternity brother, Harold, brought in a recording by a man named Earl Nightingale—a great motivational speaker. It was called *The Strangest Secret.* I listened to it over and over. He talked about having goals. And he said if I had a desire—a goal—I could have anything I wanted.

"To be honest, I wasn't quite sure I really believed all this. But I thought, *What do I have to lose?* And besides, it was adding fire to a message I'd already heard from another one of our country's greatest speakers—Dr. Norman Vincent Peale, whom I'd actually had the privilege of seeing back in Washington. His speech was based on his book, *The Power of Positive Thinking.* It seems like only yesterday . . . I bought that book and stayed up half the night reading it.

"I remember Peale saying, 'If you think in *negative* terms, you will get negative results. If you think in *positive* terms, you will achieve positive results.' Both he and Nightingale were planting these wonderful seeds in my mind. Their messages were giving me confidence."

Calvin paused, studying me carefully. Suddenly, he was asking the questions. "What about you, Stowe? Do you have goals?"

"Yes, I guess so." I squirmed, wondering what I'd say if he asked me to name them. He waited expectantly. "Well," I began, "I'd like to be healed of cancer."

"Mm, hmm . . . " He took a sip of water. "Anything else?"

"Um . . . I'd like to write some great songs . . . "

"Ok, then. That's a good start. Those are your goals. Now it's possible you may be holding a belief, somewhere deep down, that these things cannot really happen. That's normal. But what you're doing when you set your goals is to begin retraining your mind.

"Next, you need to write your goals down. This is very important and I can't emphasize it enough; *Your goals need to be written down as a constant reminder of your commitment.* I've worked with a lot of people over the years and many do not do this one simple thing . . . but it's important.

"Ok, so once you've got your goals and you've written them down, you're on your way. A person with a goal will succeed because they know where they're going—they've given their subconscious a direction.

"I remember in the recording of *The Strangest Secret*, Earl Nightingale likened our mind to a ship. He said, 'Think of a ship with the complete voyage mapped out and planned. The captain and crew know exactly where the ship is going and how long it will take—it has a definite goal. And 9,999 times out of 10,000 it will get there.'

"'Now let's take another ship—just like the first—only let's not put a crew on it, or a captain at the helm. Let's give it no aiming point, no goal, and no destination. We just start the engines and let it go. I think you'll agree that if it gets out of the harbor at all, it will either sink or wind up on some deserted beach—a derelict. It can't go anyplace because it has no destination and no guidance.'" [i]

I thought about this simple allegory—the two ships—one with a captain, one without. I hated to admit I was probably more like the second ship, somewhat aimless. But I was in a life-and-death situation now. I needed to change. I needed to be clear about my goals. "So you think I should just write down, *I want to be healed from cancer?*

"Well, that's a start . . . Only you don't want to have it out there in the future. You want to put it in the present tense. *I am healed from cancer.* Or, even better, make it positive: *I have a healthy, strong body.*

"You see, everything we observe has its origin in the mind. So you must first think of what you want. Since no one can think a thought in the future, your thought of what you desire represents its origin. But thoughts alone can only take us so far. Gregg Braden, author of *The Spontaneous Healing of Belief*, says, 'The desire or hope for a thought to come alive, without the *emotion* to give it life, is a *wish*—it's simply the image of what is possible.'

"Braden also says, 'A thought that's imbued with the power of emotion produces the feeling that brings it to life. When this happens, we've created an affirmation as well as a prayer. Both are based in feeling—and more precisely, in feeling as if the outcome has already happened. Studies have shown that the clearer and more specific we are, the greater the opportunity for a successful result.'" [ii]

"So it's the *emotion* behind what a person says that brings power to their words?"

"Yes!" Calvin beamed. "You've got it. And it's one of the two basic emotions—love or fear—that defines our beliefs. Jesus says that if you do not doubt in your heart, . . . you can ask, *believing you have already received, and it will be yours.*

"When you believe in something strongly, this belief is fueled by either love or fear. And love, of course, is the greatest of all. So I think the most important part of that command, after being bold enough to ask for something, is to *believe* and *feel in your heart* that you *already have it.*"

"It sounds like it's the opposite of, *I'll believe it when I see it.* More like, '*I'll see it when I believe it* . . .*"

"Yes," He smiled, "that's it."

I glanced at the clock; our time was almost over. But I couldn't resist one more question. "So what was your first goal?"

"First of all I asked myself, *What do I want?* Most people think, *If I just had enough money* . . . and I was really no different. Since I'd grown up without a lot of money, this thought appealed to me. I didn't have a clue as to how it was going to happen, but I set my goal: to become a millionaire . . . by the time I was thirty-five."

---

march 2, 2009

*W*E EACH HAVE GOALS *and dreams, but when and how we
reach them usually involves navigating around the many obstacles of
life—people, circumstances, illness, natural disasters, and, sometimes the biggest
stumbling block of all—ourselves. I know from experience that this last one
is a real doozy—often hindering my success—the hurdle I have faced most
in my life.*

*Now, after eleven months of dealing with a life-threatening illness, I'm
slowing down, pausing for reflection. I'm taking the opportunity to look back
over the last few years, to see what's worked and what hasn't, and to consider
how I will live out the rest of my days. Sometimes, going back in time is like
flipping through an old photo album. Sitting in the sunroom this afternoon, I
close my eyes and turn back the imaginary pages.*

*There's Peter and me on the first day we met back in 1989. Who'd have
thought we'd be together more than twenty years later? Hmm . . . look at Peter
smiling—somehow I think he knew.*

And here's me in the recording studio with one of my songwriting buddies.

I'd just had my first hit song. I was thrilled and scared, all at the same time. Could I do it again?

There's us proudly holding up Peter's first movie, Life After Life, which aired on The Learning Channel. We were so excited.

Oh, here we are in 1995. I just left the music business—almost broke my heart—after feeling like it was time for us to start a family. I'm about six months pregnant. Look how round my face is!

And there's our baby, Christina—it was love at first sight. Being parents was so much fun we wanted to do again. So here we are in 1997 with Grace, our second child.

This is Peter and me in the middle of babydom—changing diapers and throwing birthday parties, carrying little people in backpacks and reading bedtime stories. Look at my clothes! Suddenly I look like someone's mother.

My thirty-ninth birthday—I look so sad. I just found out my father has cancer and memories of my childhood begin haunting me. I fall into a deep depression. Peter's love, along with prayer and journaling, saves me.

Here we are in overalls in 2001, building our new home right after the terrorist attacks. Peter just lost the contract to renew his Hallmark TV series—his client's office was at Ground Zero. So, instead of hiring people to finish building our house, we just pick up hammers and learn to do it ourselves. What seems like a setback at first, turns out to be one of the best years of our lives.

I remember this . . . the girls and me, homeschooling on the sofa. Who'd have thought I'd ever be a homeschool mom?

Here's a photo of one of the little houses we bought in downtown Nashville. After doing renovations, we rent them out to people who qualify for Section 8. Being landlords is a long way from the creative projects we love doing, but the video and music industries almost dried up after 9/11. We had to look for other ways to make a living.

That's Peter and me, dancing at his fiftieth birthday party. Still in love, but struggling financially and creatively. We are in a typical midlife crisis, frustrated that neither of us are really doing what we were born to do.

There's a picture of me singing at a local coffee shop. I have to admit, that's where I get my greatest joy—connecting with people through music.

Boy, do I remember this, the girls and me last year—right after I found out I have cancer—trying to make some good memories on a weekend getaway.

It's been a nice, but bittersweet life review. Overall I'm encouraged, but I see plenty of room for growth. I take up Calvin's suggestion to write down my goals. I find an old notebook, one my father had used to jot down ideas, and I begin each morning by praying and setting my goals, then repeating them to myself throughout the day.

My first entry:

I will spend more time with my family. I want to enjoy our days together, talking, playing, listening.

I will write at least one song a month.

I will be healed of cancer. I believe this is possible.

I am healed. I am healed. I am healed.

∾ flying high ∾

learning
the ropes

Every battle is won before it is fought.

—SUN TZU

An old black-and-white photo hung in the corner of Calvin's office, a newspaper clipping that had been enlarged to show two young men in the heat of a boxing moment. Two things stood out; the large bulbous glove of an unseen boxer in the forefront and, just inches from it, the image of an open-mouthed young man reeling from a great blow to the chin. It was Calvin.

Calvin told me about his days in the ring and what he learned about the *power of thought*. I tried to imagine him as a boxer. He was in good shape now for a man his age—not Mohammad Ali shape—but that's because he didn't continue boxing and his muscles stopped memorizing the contours of a boxer's body. His experience in the ring did, however, have a great affect on his *mind* muscle—the most powerful of all.

I imagined him in the fall of 1955.

He stands at the sink, gazing into the hazy locker room mirror, a young man of seventeen. Staring at his reflection, he somehow senses life has passed him by—especially where sports are concerned. Not that he hasn't made the effort. The fact is, he's tried out for everything Franklin High has to offer. And he's failed.

There are only two things he knows for sure—he isn't tall enough for basketball and he isn't big enough for football. So, shoving his hands into his pockets, he takes one last look in the mirror and walks away, convinced he is a nobody; a loser.

Wearing the crown of self-pity is not Calvin's destiny though. This autumn season brings with it the winds of change. Franklin High starts a boxing team and for the first time in a long time Calvin's thoughts turn hopeful. *Boxing. This could be my salvation.*

He signs up the next day. Fueled by spit and determination, he hits the ring. He eats, sleeps, and breathes boxing. *Get into your stance. Left knee at twelve o'clock, toe at one. Right foot behind. C'mon now. It's all about balance. Elbows in, fists up. Extend the arm, corkscrew out. Punch the bag. Good left hook. Yeah, that's it. Keep your hands high. Now throw that jab.* Aching arms. *Keep moving. Bob and duck.* Tired legs. *Breathe. There you go, there you go. That's good.*

Before long, Calvin is boxing and he is scheduled for his first of two fights. This initial battle, with its unforgettable images and feelings, will leave an indelible mark on the man Calvin later becomes.

The big event finally arrives. Out in the parking lot, strains of Elvis Presley's "Don't Be Cruel" wafts from a car radio. Calvin walks to the beat, his hands clenched.

Descending the concrete stairway that leads into the front of the gym, he passes through the fluorescent-lit halls. He walks with his head tilted slightly upward and stares at the hard-won trophies and photos of former football and basketball players. Darris McCord. Gentry Roberts. Crawford Alexander. The images are mesmerizing—heroes forever frozen in glorious mid-air poses. He dares to dream. *Maybe . . . maybe one day I'll be up there . . .*

Remembering his destination, he hurries toward his future. A door opens. He takes a deep breath, walks into the humid locker room, and readies himself for battle. Followed by his coach, he soon emerges wearing red boxing shorts and gloves. Together they step into the arena—a noisy gymnasium. Another deep breath.

As the coach tapes his hands, Calvin scans the gym for his opponent. Then he sees him, bouncing effortlessly from foot to foot. He has the look of a street fighter—focused, self-assured—with thick, meaty arms jabbing confidently at the air. Watching him, fear floods Calvin's body. His knees shake. "Coach . . . "

"Yeah," he puts the final tape on Calvin's knuckles.

"Coach, I can't beat *him* . . . " He stares down at his trainer, hoping that somehow he can get out of the fight. "I've *seen* him, Coach. He beats up guys in *and* out of the ring."

Calvin summons his powers of visualization. Only he imagines his *opponent* winning the match. Watching the other fighter shadowboxing is all it takes for Calvin to see himself defeated . . . a loser again.

Now he is in the ring. The bell sounds and his opponent is on the attack. *Punch. Umpf!* Calvin's head spins; his jaw aches.

From the corner, he hears his coach. "Keep your hands up, boy! Chin down!" Calvin punches wildly. His legs are weak. The assault continues. The bell rings. Now, dizzy and confused, the coach helps him down from the ring. His vision now a painful reality. Calvin was beaten before the fight ever began.

With the sting of losing, Calvin is more than ready to hang up his boxing gloves for good. But the next fight is already scheduled. Reluctantly, he agrees to honor his commitment, while inside he dreads another beating.

"I don't think I'm cut out to be a boxer, Coach . . ." He assumes his trainer will agree. Instead, Coach Sutton says something he will never forget.

"Calvin, you have a good left jab."

"I don't even remember hitting the guy." Calvin is dumbfounded. " . . . a good left jab?"

"Mmm, hmm, and that's what we're going to work on."

Sometimes a simple word of praise can make all the difference in the world between success and failure. It is this one, sincere compliment, like soothing balm for his bruised ego, that grows in Calvin's mind and gives him confidence.

I've got a good left jab becomes his mantra. Like a computer receiving an update to the hard drive, Calvin's mind reprograms for success. At his second fight, Calvin is honing the mental focus that will eventually take him far into the future. He is nervous, of course. He has no idea who he is up against. But he knows one thing for certain—he gets a point for every time he hits his opponent.

The bell rings. The crowd cheers. Calvin, focused, is moving in on his opponent, jabbing his left arm constantly. As he bobs and weaves around his rival, the audience stamps their feet in appreciation. *Defend, counter, attack. I've got a good left jab.* Each punch energizes him. He is fearless. He is in the moment. The bell sounds.

And the winner is . . . Calvin LeHew!

"Coach, did you *see it*? Did you see how I *hit* him?"

"Yeah, Calvin. I saw you!"

Calvin learned later that his foe was a greater fighter than his first opponent. When he was challenged to a rematch, Calvin didn't even have to think about it, he accepted. Newfound confidence coupled with his old country grit gave him all the courage he needed. *I beat him once; I can beat him again.*

And he did.

dreams
take flight

*A journey of a thousand miles begins with that first
and all-important single step.*

—LAO TZU

Calvin and I walked down one of the long corridors of The Factory to the Stoveworks Restaurant. Today, instead of Calvin's office, Peter asked us to meet there. He wanted to film us.

After the crew finished setting up the lights, the camera began rolling. I was eager to hear how the story of Calvin's quest to become a millionaire by age thirty-five unfolded.

"Alright . . . " I tried to ignore the camera. "Your life has been one success after another. One of the first things I'd like to know is . . . how'd you do it?"

Calvin leaned forward, his elbows on the table, "You know a lot of folks think you have to be an expert at something to be successful. But that's not necessarily true. And you don't need to have a high IQ. I surely don't!

"All you need are a goal and a belief. To be honest, much of my success has come from not knowing any better. I didn't have the fear of failure that plagues so many people. I didn't *know* what I was getting into when I started a drugstore chain, so the positive principles I talk about worked for me. You've got to walk right into what you *want* and not look at what you don't want. Stay focused on the goal."

"So . . . a goal and a belief," I made a note on a small legal pad. "You say those are really the keys to success . . . What else would you tell people who are starting out in business?"

"I'd tell them a couple of things: First, always give more than is expected of you— "

I repeated and wrote. "Give . . . more than . . . expected . . . "

"Absolutely!" He tapped his finger on the table. "To me, this is the most important principle . . . give *more* than is expected. Also, another way to be successful is to be *different*. Don't copy anybody else.

"These two principles are the reasons I was able to reach my goal of becoming a millionaire. It all started one night in a restaurant in Knoxville, Tennessee, when I was having dinner with my fraternity brother and soon-to-be business partner, Harold Pierce. He was the guy who turned me on to the motivational speaker, Earl Nightingale—and now we were preparing to go into business together. We just hadn't figured out what *kind* yet."

"Calvin . . . " Harold began. "I talked to the vice-president of Jerry's Restaurant today. He says Tallahassee, Florida, would be a great town to open a Jerry's. It's such a popular chain. Would you be open to looking into that?"

"Sure!"

"I know we don't know a thing about the restaurant business . . . "

"Shoot," Calvin threw up both hands. "We don't know a thing about *any* business. But that won't stop us . . . the food will sell itself."

"How about we take a trip down there and check it out?"

A week later Calvin and Harold toured the town of Tallahassee, talking about the possibilities of owning a restaurant. But after several months of research, they found that financing a commercial restaurant just wasn't possible for two young college graduates. Undaunted, they continued exploring Tallahassee, dreaming about a business that could succeed there. Walking the streets, they had only one question in mind: *What does this town need?*

They quickly figured it out.

"Harold . . . I haven't seen one single discount drugstore around here."

"Hey, you're right!" Harold snapped his fingers. "Remember those discount drugstores they have up north? They are really successful— "

"And it doesn't take as much up-front capital to start one of those either."

"Right . . . And Florida State University would be *great* for business!"

Calvin elbowed his partner. "Harold, I think you're onto something."

" . . . And that's how we started." Calvin crossed his hands in his lap. "We opened our first drugstore and decided to discount every item, every day by at least twenty percent. Back in those days, continual deep discounts were unusual. And here we were discounting *every* item *every* day—cigarettes, chewing gum, cold drinks—you name it. We even had the vending machines made differently so they reflected a twenty percent discount. You see? We were *giving more than expected.*"

Calvin remembers the day Harold held up their accounting books for him to see. "Look at this! I can't get over how well we're doing. I mean, most stores are marking up everything forty percent, but we're only getting twenty—obviously, we have to sell twice as many goods to make the same profit. But here we are, not only selling twice as many goods, we're selling three, four, and even five times as many! We're getting rich . . . selling *hairspray.*"

"Who said we needed to be experts in the drugstore business?"

The front door opened with its familiar *ding* as Calvin and Harold looked up to see six pretty coeds from Florida State University stroll in the door.

"Hi, boys!" They giggled and headed for the cosmetics counter.

"And there's our main customer, buddy." Harold winked at Calvin. "*They're* the reason we're in business."

" . . . It was quite a ride for two young college grads," Calvin continued. "I'll tell you, our competitors hated us. They literally tried to run us out of town! All because we did *more* than customers *expected*. Well, once we got the Tallahassee drugstore up and running, we immediately opened another in Albany, Georgia; then Dothan, Alabama; and one in Gainesville, Florida.

"A big lesson was drilled into me during those early Tallahassee days . . . *you have to give in order to receive*—that rule applies if you're selling a product, a service, or if you're in any other kind of relationship. We didn't make this up; and it didn't just come from our business. In fact, it really hit home in our Ten Brave Christians Bible study group."

"Ten Brave Christians?" We seemed to have taken a sudden detour from business to religion. "What was that?"

"Stowe, that was an experience that changed my life."

———— ⊗⊗⊗ ————

ten brave christians

Only a life lived for others is worth living.

—ALBERT EINSTEIN

We paid our bill at the Stoveworks and walked upstairs to Calvin's office. I was curious to hear about this life changing experience from over forty years ago.

"Ten Brave Christians . . . " he began, "was a phenomenon—sort of a revival that swept through the South many years ago. And Marilyn and I were two of the first Ten." He paused, and I wondered if he was studying my reaction to see if I wanted to hear more about his personal religious experience. I smiled, encouraging him to go on.

"It happened while Marilyn and I lived in Tallahassee and it was definitely life-changing . . . it had a profound effect on my faith and beliefs."

"What kind of church were you attending?

"A Methodist Church. But it wasn't the old-style, hell-fire-and-damnation kind of Methodist Church that scared me as a child. I really tried to distance myself from that. By the time we moved to Tallahassee, I'd learned more of the positive sorts of teachings of Jesus from

Reverend Peale. That's when Marilyn and I discovered the John Wesley Methodist Church."

Calvin reached into a drawer and pulled out a ragged paperback. He aimed the cover in my direction and I read, "A Life That Really Matters, by Danny Morris."

"He was our pastor and he wrote this book, telling how the Ten Brave Christians—sometimes called The Great John Wesley Experiment—came to be. It was a story about how God touched a whole lot of people through a man named Sam Teague.

"It began when Sam, our Sunday school teacher for the young adults class, had an amazing experience. He wanted to share it with our church. But first, he asked our pastor, Danny Morris, to prepare us for it. He called it The Ten Brave Christians Experiment and for the next five Sundays, pastor Morris highlighted one of the five specific principles that Sam felt would not only improve our lives, but also give us a closer relationship with God. Each step was carefully laid out to prepare our hearts for the question Sam would ask on the sixth Sunday. I remember it like it was yesterday.

"Sam Teague carried a large yellow pad and smiled nervously as he stepped to the platform to take pastor Morris's place that Sunday morning. He stood behind the podium, holding the sides of it for support, cleared his throat, and looked out across the parishioners. The room fell silent. Sam took a deep breath and in a shaky, soft-spoken voice, began to tell a very personal story.

"'My friends, it is because I care deeply for you that I am here today. Many of you are in my young adult's class but I want you to know that this message is for everyone.' Marilyn and I exchanged glances, wondering what he was going to talk about.

"'For several months now, my heart has been troubled. I've tried so hard . . . but it feels like I haven't been getting through to you. I see you all just going through the motions. But your lives, your priorities . . . well . . .' Sam took a deep breath. 'They seem . . . shallow. Please don't misunderstand—I don't say this in a judgmental sort of way. It's just that many of you have shared with me your goals and dreams. And they are *of this world*—money, cars, vacations, and houses—not bad things . . . but friends, there is so much more that God wants for you.

"'One Sunday last month I went to the bank where I work. I often do this on Sunday morning, to prepare for class. I was discouraged. So I put my head down on my desk and, with an aching heart, I desperately asked God to help me show these young people how to live *a life that really matters*.' He clenched his folded hand to his heart, obviously drawn with emotion.

"'Those were my exact words: Help me show these young people how to live a life that really matters. And then . . . something exciting happened!' Sam's countenance raised a noticeable notch.

"'I began receiving a fully-formed idea—it was like taking dictation. So, I got out my legal pad and started writing it all down.' He picked up a legal pad from the podium for all to see. 'This went on for about twenty minutes. And then it shut off . . .' He snapped his fingers. 'Just like that. It's a work that I feel is literally straight from God.'

"Sam looked out into the crowd and, in a voice now strong and sure, said, 'Friends, I need ten volunteers to join me for an experiment. I only want those who are sincere and will commit to doing five things for the month of March:

1. Meet once a week to pray together
2. Give two hours time each week to God
3. Give God one-tenth of their earnings
4. Spend from 5:30 to 6:00 each morning in prayer, meditation, and writing down goals
5. Witness for God their experiences to others'

"Sam paused, scanning the congregation. 'Who will join me and commit to living a life that really matters? Can I get a show of hands?'

"Well, Stowe, you know I'm an adventurous type and I've always liked new challenges, so I was one of the first to raise my hand."

"How about Marilyn?"

"Well, she wasn't quite sure she wanted to at first . . . we had to talk about it later, but she did agree eventually. It turned out joining that group was one of the greatest things that ever happened to me.

"We began each morning by reading certain verses from the Bible—verses Sam had been inspired to pick out—which taught us *how to pray.* Then we wrote down what it meant to us in our lives.

"Sam also instructed us to do one unselfish deed for someone every day and keep a journal of it. It was interesting to me how difficult it was to do an unselfish deed every day, something you don't get any benefit from.

"I remember one of my deeds . . . It was back in the mid-sixties, you know, during the civil rights era, and we were having racial conflicts in Tallahassee. I was at the post office one day when I saw an African American lady with her hands full of packages. I ran right past her, up the steps, and opened the door for her. This simple act of kindness was a bit unusual for that time. I'll never forget how surprised she was that I would go out of my way to help her! But it made me feel good inside. It was such a minor thing but it added to my *aliveness* that day. So I tried to do more things like that.

"That month transformed me . . . and our church, too. We met and prayed once a week for folks who had problems with their marriages, with money, health, and alcohol. And *miracles* happened. People were getting well. Money came in when needed. Marriages were saved. This book, *A Life That Really Matters*, tells about those miracles, and how people's lives were changed."

Calvin handed the book to me and I flipped it open to a dog-eared page. The names *Calvin* and *Marilyn* jumped out at me. I read their brief testimony, which Danny Morris included, among many others.

"One of our most memorable tithing stories was shared at our first meeting. Marilyn and Calvin were a young couple, struggling over whether to be in our first group. Sam and I had announced on Sunday that anyone who signed up that morning or mailed in their commitment form, postmarked before midnight on Monday, would be in the group. Thereafter, the group would be closed for the month. Calvin had gone home for lunch on Monday and he and Marilyn had one final discussion over the last point of their struggle: Could they give a tenth of their [considerable] income for the month? They figured out the dollar amount and decided to take the step of faith. They signed the commitment and sealed the stamped envelope just as they heard the postman coming.

Marilyn quickly flipped through the mail before Calvin left for work and noticed an unusual envelope. She opened it and found a letter from a man who had owed them money from a couple of years earlier. Long ago they had concluded he would never repay them. The man had written to apologize for the delay in paying and included a check. The check was for the exact amount of the monthly tithe they had just computed before signing their commitment form.

At this point in their story they were both in tears of awe and joy, as were many in our group. Calvin told us something we would all come to experience: "We may find it is hard to out-give God!" [iii]

I studied Calvin, the same man Danny Morris wrote about forty years ago, and I realized how this lesson had echoed throughout his and Marilyn's life together. Known for their great generosity, I couldn't help but wonder if they were still trying to out-give God.

"It's so important to *give*," he said, "and to give something of *value*. It doesn't matter if it's money or helping the needy with your time, serving meals, or reading to kids. When you change your attitude about giving—well, something amazing happens."

I pushed the book back across the table. Calvin laid his hand on the cover. "I learned so much from that experience, like writing down goals about how we wished to be used by God. It sounds simple, but it's extremely important.

"And praying with other people . . . Like Jesus says, 'Where two or more are gathered together in My name, there I will be also.' Prayer is a wonderful power we can use. But if we're thinking negative, selfish thoughts, we cut ourselves off from that power. So we have to meditate on positive things that give us hope."

Looking at Calvin, I imagined a kind of Rubik's Cube of his multi-faceted life story—the twists and turns all added up to a pattern that defied one single box of philosophy or religious doctrine. But they seemed to be a system of beliefs and principles that had obviously worked for him.

"There's an infinite intelligence out there, greater than we are, that loves us and wants the best for us . . . some people call it God or Holy Spirit. Whatever you choose to call it we can use this, and be used by it, for our benefit and for the benefit of others. And that's when we see the miracles! God, in his infinite love and wisdom, can bring about these things for us if we have enough faith and belief. It's what Jesus tries to teach us when He says, 'These things you can do and even greater.'

"But it takes spending time with God, strengthening our connection, and learning his will for us." He opened his hands and looked to the ceiling. "' . . . be ye transformed by the renewing of your mind that ye may prove what is the good and acceptable and perfect will of God.'"

march 16, 2009

L ATE INTO THE NIGHT *with just the glow of our alarm clock to light our bedroom, Peter and I lie awake talking about the Ten Brave Christians experience. I can hear in his voice how it moved him. Calvin's own testimony about prayer and tithing revealed some important clues about his life's driving force. And then there was the divinely inspired writing of Sam Teague—that was definitely an unusual experience.*

Peter's spiritual lights are turned on. "Calvin told me yesterday that the Ten Brave Christians was the most important experience of his whole life. He said it was the beginning of his 'Christ-Consciousness.'"

"It really affected him, didn't it?"

"Yes . . . and just hearing him tell about it . . . somehow it makes me appreciate him even more."

"Do you identify with him?"

"In a way. You know, he's definitely an out of the box *thinker, some might even say a contradiction in terms. Here he sets out to be a millionaire, then has this spiritual experience—pursuing a life that really matters—but ends*

up with the money anyway. And this Ten Brave Christians experience seems to have grounded him in biblical fundamentals, then he goes on to study books on metaphysics, quantum physics, body-mind-spirit healing, fire walking, etc.

"So yes, in some ways . . . you know, it's kind of how I've walked the tightrope between fundamental Christian doctrines and what people call 'new thought' spirituality. I've done it for years and it's not easy. I'm a follower of Jesus, after my own Christ-encounter, yet my films tend to deal with more unconventional heavenly phenomena . . . like the angels and miracles, and especially the near-death experiences. And, like Calvin, I don't always speak in Christian-ese to express the deep spiritual truths of Jesus . . . "

There is a brief moment of quiet and I find myself thinking about Calvin. He really does seem to follow God's guidance in a . . . personal way.

Peter and I agree that God reaches out to people wherever they happen to be on life's path, in places where we ourselves may have once been or may one day be. And we are both pretty open-minded to expanding our spiritual understanding. So it's no surprise to me when Peter says he wants to start a Ten Brave Christians group, to see firsthand what Calvin experienced.

"I want to find a copy of the book, A Life That Really Matters, so I can study it. I have a feeling it'll give us a better understanding of Calvin."

Little does he know, but Peter is about to experience his own installment of one of Calvin's synchronicities, or so-called meaningful coincidences.

Only days later, Peter is killing some time between appointments in a grocery store across town. "Hey . . . Peter Shockey!" a voice calls from the end of the produce aisle.

My husband turns to greet Andy Miller, an old friend from the publishing business. They haven't seen each other in years. After quickly catching up on highlights, Peter mentions doing a book project with Calvin LeHew.

Andy jumps in. "Oh sure, I know Calvin . . . owner of The Factory. Well, that's interesting you're working with him. My latest client just happens to be an old friend of his from forty years ago!"

"Really?" Peter nods, not quite making the connection. But Andy's next line makes Peter's jaw drop.

"Yeah . . . a Methodist pastor named Danny Morris. He wrote a book called A Life That Really Matters.*"*

"You're kidding . . . I've been wanting to get a copy of that book!"

"Yeah? Well, I just picked up the republishing rights to it. How many do you want?"

A few days later Peter comes home with a dozen complimentary copies of A Life That Really Matters. *He puts the word out to our Sunday school group, and within a few weeks we start our own Ten Brave Christians study. On our first of four Sunday nights together, we realize that we are coincidentally starting on the first week in March, just like the original group had done over forty years ago. Peter volunteers to lead the sessions, which he begins with a simple prayer, asking God to guide us through the series.*

In a way, we are time traveling. We start each morning with one of the Bible readings Sam Teague picked out for Calvin and Marilyn's class nearly a half century earlier. Then, according to the original "dictated" instructions, we spend the next ten minutes in meditation on that scripture. Altogether, the main teachings from these scriptural texts are aimed at learning how to pray.

Therefore I tell you, whatever you ask for in prayer, believe that you have received it, and it will be yours—Mark 11:24. *We taste for ourselves the spiritual food that nourished the younger Calvin. These biblical foundations validate the principles he already learned, like the power of positive thinking.*

*We are encouraged again to trust that answers will come—*Ask and it will be given to you; seek and you will find; knock and the door will be opened to you—*Luke 11:9-10.*

*And on facing fear, we are reminded—*Do not let your hearts be troubled. Trust in God; trust also in me—*John 14:1.*

*We understand why Calvin is so hungry to study and practice God's principles of running the universe. He still studies every morning, often long before 5:30—*Blessed is the man who does not walk in the counsel of the wicked . . . But his delight is in the law of the LORD, and on his law he meditates day and night. He is like a tree planted by streams of water, which yields its fruit in season and whose leaf does not wither. Whatever he does prospers—*Psalm 1:1-3*.

And perhaps most evident in his and Marilyn's lives, even after forty years . . . let your light shine before men, that they may see your good deeds and praise your Father in heaven—*Matthew 5:16*.

Peter and I, along with our friends, learn many priceless lessons during the month-long study. Lessons like writing down our goals for how God can use us. And meditating—not just asking of God, but taking time to quietly listen. And doing unselfish acts of service for others, not only giving financially, but also of our time. And in the tradition of the earliest gatherings, our group decides to keep on meeting and praying. They have been among our most faithful friends who keep my family and me lifted up in prayer over my health issues.

Good lessons. I'm learning something from Calvin's experiences. And this last one—discovering how to live a life that really matters—is especially timely. None of us know how long we'll walk this world, but there's one thing I do know—I want to make whatever time I have left count.

a woman
named bonnie

Success is a tale of obstacles overcome, and for every
obstacle overcome, an excuse not used.

—ROBERT BRAULT

Rounding the corner into Calvin's office I got the immediate impression he had a bit of spring fever. The big window was open, allowing a sweet breeze to flow through the room. Calvin told us he'd woken up especially early this morning—2:30! He found his early reading time very meaningful. He also informed us he'd been invited to speak to a group later that afternoon.

"Do you have a speech planned?"

"No," he shrugged. "Not really. I usually just jot down a few notes beforehand, but my intention is always to encourage folks any way I can. Sometimes I just ask people, 'What would you do if you knew you could not fail?' It makes no difference how outrageous it might be. What would you do if you knew you could not fail?"

I thought about it. "It's really liberating, isn't it?"

"It is." He stretched and put his hands behind his head. "The first time I read that in a book I said, 'Man, I would soar like an eagle!' So I took up hang gliding about two weeks later. Went right down to

Mexico and never looked back. You see that one little question—*what would you do if you knew you could not fail?*—puts life in a different perspective. Most people make excuses. They use their gender, lack of money, health, or their education level as reasons why they can't live the life of their dreams. And I'll tell you there are a lot of people out there using age as an excuse.

"I remember hearing about Harland Sanders—the founder of Kentucky Fried Chicken or KFC. He'd already been in the restaurant business for a while but he was in his early sixties when he achieved his great success. How about that? Age certainly wasn't a factor for him.

"But the one experience I had that made me swear off excuses for good happened back when I took a visit to Goodwill Industries in St. Petersburg, Florida. I met a woman there named Bonnie and I've never felt sorry for myself since. The first time I saw her sitting on a stool, I was immediately struck by the fact that she had no arms whatsoever, not even a nub. And guess what kind of job she had?"

I shook my head, unable to imagine what this woman would be able to do.

"She was a telephone switchboard operator."

My eyes widened. "An *operator*? "

"Yes. And she did it with no hands or arms—she worked that switchboard with her toes! I'll tell you, I just watched in awe at what this lady was doing. There she was, writing and taking messages with her feet. And even more amazing was that she taught herself how to do this. I was pretty impressed!

"Soon it was lunchtime and I wondered, *How's she going to eat?* No sooner had I thought this, someone pushed a lunch tray in front of her and she brought her feet up to the table, took her knife and fork, and began feeding herself! Her muscles and legs were so limber, she could actually do that. Afterwards, she lit up a cigarette— struck the match all by herself. 'Bonnie,' I said, 'is there *anything* you can't do?'

"She shook her head. 'Up until last week I thought I couldn't hang up my clothes to dry at home. But my husband, who's in a wheelchair, solved that problem.' She told me how he rigged up a pulley outside. They put a sheet on the ground, put their clothes on the sheet and then let the clothesline down to the ground. Next, Bonnie pinned the clothes on the line and, finally, pulled the line up so they could dry. Now, *that* lady was not handicapped!

"It just makes me wonder, how many of us go through life with what we think are handicaps? We've always got an excuse for why we can't soar like eagles . . . "

Listening to Calvin I thought about how, all too often, I made excuses for why I couldn't soar like an eagle. I'd been given my own set of wings. In fact, God had blessed me in so many ways that could have sent me flying higher than I could ever imagine. Yet, somehow, I managed to stay earthbound, keeping myself prisoner in an invisible cage and never realizing the only thing holding me back was me.

"Calvin, do you think anybody ever fulfills their potential?"

His eyes were soft with understanding. "I think we're just not aware of how much we *can* do. What comes to my mind is what Jesus says . . . *'these things you can do and even greater.'* Why aren't more people doing *these things?* I don't know for sure . . . but Jesus was the Christ—he embodied the Christ-mind—and everything He did came from a place of unconditional love. His miracles weren't about His power, but about His love. And I believe that as brothers and sisters of Jesus, when we conform to the mind of Christ we also have the ability to express unconditional love. Unfortunately, we tend to do things from a place of ego. *What's in it for me?*"

He pointed to his heart. " . . . At least I do."

I nodded and we sat quietly for a minute.

Finally, Calvin said, "Meeting Bonnie changed me. After that I realized my goal to become a millionaire was shallow, and that living a life that mattered meant more than just chasing after money. I didn't have any excuses anymore for why I couldn't succeed at whatever I was led to do."

It was time for me to go, so we gave each other a hug. "See you next week." I headed into the hallway, walked a few steps, then glanced back at him. This experience—helping him write his book—was supposed to be a professional venture. I always put my heart and soul into every song, every book I write, but I've done so with the knowledge that ultimately, it's my profession. How could I have known when I took on this project that I would be so affected by Calvin's stories . . . that my life would change in so many ways, just by hearing and recording his? It felt like a grand orchestration of events designed to open my eyes and make me examine myself. And it was in the spirit of that unconditional love of Christ that I felt suddenly overwhelmed with appreciation for him.

"Hey, Calvin . . . " I said softly. "I love you." It was the first time I ever told him this.

There was a pause—I don't think he expected such a show of emotion. He smiled. And then, I heard him, "Love you, too."

homecoming

Circumstances do not make the man, they reveal him.

—James Allen

Being a part of the Ten Brave Christians was the beginning of a transformation in Calvin's life. But just as a sailboat tacks back and forth, zigzagging to its destination, so did Calvin. He was now a husband in his early thirties, a successful businessman, and also a seeker who wanted to do something meaningful with his life. He didn't know exactly what that was yet, but two things seemed clear: he was excited by the idea of helping others learn to help themselves; and he realized that every journey begins with a first step.

"So what was your next move?" I asked.

"I began by selling out my share of the drugstore business to my partner, Harold. Then I became a member of the board of directors at Goodwill Industries. I really liked they way they operated, like how they were into recycling—taking old things, fixing them up, and then reselling them—this philosophy resonated strongly within me. It was their policy to hire people who needed jobs as well as those who were handicapped, mentally or physically, like Bonnie. All of this excited me and I felt the Spirit leading me into the desire to do more things like this.

"It was an interesting time . . . seeing this *shift* in my thinking. I wanted to make a fresh start, so I checked into becoming an executive with Goodwill Industries. That didn't work out but it made me realize I was open to something that would be a higher and better use of my life.

"So here I was, out of work and exploring other careers—some of which were quite unusual. It was around this time that I realized my young wife, Marilyn, was beginning to think I'd lost my marbles. I think she was wondering what had happened to her ambitious husband . . . so we moved back to Franklin, Tennessee."

I nodded. "You probably wanted to keep things secure for her . . . "

"Yes, I did. So when we got home, I called my brother-in-law, Kenneth Holt, who's a great carpenter, and I talked him into going into the contracting business. Now I'm here to tell you, I couldn't build a doghouse!" Calvin's voice rose comically. "But I'd made up my mind what I wanted to do. So I got a general contractor's license and the next thing I knew I was off chasing a new dream."

I tilted my head, surprised by this direction. "Wasn't that kind of a departure . . . you know, from your goal of trying to live a life that matters?"

"In some ways it was . . . but, in hindsight, I can see it was all part of the journey, part of learning what I needed to know so I could do greater things later on. In a way, I was just spreading my wings, learning to fly.

"We started out small, bought our first lot for $2,500. Then we built a $14,000 house on it, sold it, and made a $500 profit."

I did a double take. "That's not much money . . . "

"Nope. But when you begin something new you've got to get from here to there, and the way you do that is by building confidence in yourself bit by bit. I'd never built houses before so I was learning as I went.

"But along the way, I was learning some other very important lessons—like how powerful our imagination is and how important it is to surround yourself with people who are smarter than you, people who can help you achieve your goal. I always remind folks to reward the people on their team. I've heard that you cannot enrich yourself without enriching others first."

As I listened to Calvin, I realized he was a vivid example of a great achiever; not someone who necessarily does so much—but someone around whom things get done. His energy stirs others to greatness.

Through the small opening in the wall, where Calvin exchanges documents with his management team, I heard the happy voices of Rod, Tammy, and Jack—his dedicated team—those whom Calvin gives credit for really running The Factory.

Across from me, Calvin rummaged through his drawer. "Ah, here it is." He handed me a photo of himself at a *Holt & LeHew Construction* building site. Dark-haired, wearing a shirt and tie, and holding a ruler toward a new house, he appeared to be instructing a carpenter. "That's me when we were just starting out. Eventually, we became the largest custom homebuilder in Williamson County.

"It was around that time I began to realize how all the positive principles I'd studied for so many years were working for me. I could see in my balance sheets that I was making a profit each month. So I decided to step up the pace.

"We bought some land and built a subdivision of thirty-seven lots. Now I could really see my goals becoming a reality."

"That must've been so exciting."

"It was . . . but at the same time it was kind of frightening. You see, sometimes success scares you because you haven't had it before. It may seem strange, but we can actually have a *fear of success*."

"You don't strike me as someone who's afraid of success."

He laughed. "Well, let's put it this way, I didn't let it stop me. I was on a roll now, caught up in the excitement of how well everything was working. I wanted to do something even more daring. And I had a big idea. I wanted to build something—a shopping center like no one had done before."

I shook my head and stared at Calvin. That was a bold-sounding dream. I wondered, *had he lost his vision? Or had he found it?*

∞ flying high ∞

the voice
within

Prayer is when you talk to God; meditation is when you listen.

—Diana Robinson

Today Peter and I took a trip out to Calvin's favorite place—his farm. He stood beside an old tobacco barn as we pulled in. I waved to him. Moments later, the two of us ambled along together through the tall grass while Peter filmed us. The light of the afternoon sun cast a golden glow around Calvin and his dogs, illuminating a multitude of flying bugs. He'd just shown me his new helicopter, a one-man flying machine. He called the small craft *The Mosquito*. Looking at it, I had to laugh. Compared with all the other mosquitoes around here, it was a monster.

I wondered where this love affair with flying machines began.

"Oh, I've always been fascinated with it, ever since I was a kid." He swatted a bug. "The first time I flew in an airplane was back in 1952 when my father took me to Washington, D.C., to Senator Gore's inauguration . . . "

"So why didn't you become a professional pilot?"

"That's a good question . . . " he squinted at the sky. "I was definitely headed in that direction . . . "

"What happened?"

"It was at the end of summer camp at Reese Air Force Base . . . and I was the top commander of my cadet group when I was called up for an award. I loved flying. And up until that moment, I'd planned to make it my life. But as I stepped up before the review board to receive my award, something happened that shocked everyone in the room, including me.

"'Mr. LeHew,' Commander Moon began. 'You *do* expect to make a career out of the Air Force, don't you?'

"'No, sir . . . I really don't.'

"I was stunned when those words came out of my mouth. No one in the room could have been any more surprised than me. I don't even remember what happened afterwards. I only know that the course of my life changed forever that day.

"Where do you think that answer came from?"

"I honestly don't know. But I've wondered many times over the years what caused me to say that. It was almost as if something took over me, something from a deeper spiritual place . . . I think of it as *the voice within*."

We continued traipsing through the high grasses, our conversation going from deeply spiritual to shallow, schoolyard teasing. Months of hanging around together had put us at ease and we enjoyed bouncing around ideas and sharing our struggles. Calvin had become someone I confided in—a mentor, and a friend.

"Calvin, you've done a lot and overcome so much in your life, like the doubts of bankers and naysayers. And that story you just told about the voice within . . . that speaks to me."

"Mm hm . . . "

"Can I ask you something?"

"I'm all ears," he said.

"I grew up with lots of mixed messages, which I internalized as doubts about my abilities. I'm wondering . . . how does a person get past the *negative* voices?"

"Don't listen to them."

"I know that's what I *should* do . . . but it's not always easy."

"Well, first of all, don't go 'shoulding' on yourself . . . " He winked.

"Yeah, yeah . . . " I groaned.

"First of all, just know you're not alone. There've been lots of folks who've struggled with negative voices and they got past them by staying focused on what they wanted. I remember I read a story in the L.A. Times once. It's a good example of what I'm talking about. A young man had gone to a dance. From across the room he saw a beautiful woman. It took a while but he finally worked up the courage to ask her to dance. He was so excited when she said 'yes.' But after a few minutes she crushed him with just a few words.

"'You're a lousy dancer,' she complained. 'You dance like a truck driver.' Can you imagine someone telling you that?"

"Ouch . . . "

"Yeah, it hurt. Now a lot of folks would've gone home and never danced again—just put their feet up on the coffee table and watched television. But this young man didn't let it stop him. He had a *passion* for dancing.

"In fact, this man became known as one of the greatest dancers of the 20th century. He had a television show, which aired for eleven years, teaching people from all walks of life—including truck drivers—how to dance. And, by the time of his death, in the early nineties, he had five hundred dance schools named after him . . . "

"Are you talking about *Arthur Murray*?"

"That's the man . . . he ignored the negative voices and just did what he loved to do."

"How inspiring . . . "

"It is. But, remember, it's not just *negative* comments we have to get out of our head. Sometimes people think they're encouraging us—and they can be very strong in their convictions about how they see us—when, in fact, their aspirations for us might be off target. I'll tell you about something that happened to me when I was young.

"After my father died I felt lost and afraid. It seemed as though everyone had left me. I wondered, *What am I going to do with my life?* Then one day I ran into Emory Jones, the man who'd kept the books at my father's old sawmill. He was someone I admired and, shaking his hand, I realized how glad I was to see him again. He wanted to know what I was going to do with my life. . . I told him I didn't know.

"Mr. Jones put his hand on my shoulder and said, 'Calvin, I've seen you around the sawmill—you've got a knack for tinkering with fans and gasoline engines and such. Now that's a talent you can use.'"

"'Really . . .' I felt somehow flattered and discouraged at the same time. It wasn't exactly the kind of life I had envisioned. 'You think so?'

"'He nodded authoritatively. 'Son, what you need to do is go up to Hillsboro'—back then this was a little village with a population of no more than twenty-five, counting the dogs—' . . . and rent you out a building and open up a little electronic shop. Then you can work on fans and toasters . . . things like that. Earn a nice little living. And later, marry a local girl, have a family.' He was very persistent in this.

"I almost listened to this man, who believed that was the height to which I could go in life. Fortunately, I didn't take Mr. Jones's advice. Something inside told me it wasn't the way to go. I took my time in making my choices. I went off by myself and listened to that *still, small voice* within. What I found over the years is that it's okay to listen to the opinions of others but always go *inside* for true guidance."

We continued walking in silence, enjoying the peaceful sounds of the crickets and birds, the wind in the trees. His words made sense to me, and I felt my spirit relax in the calming environment. It was good to be away from the noise of the modern world, the TV news with all its doom and gloom, and the mindless chatter of life.

But, still, I wondered, "How do you get away from the constant stream of thought?"

"Just let them go . . . take your time . . . quiet your mind and *listen* to the stillness within. That's where you find the voice of God."

april 13, 2009

I DO BELIEVE *in going within—to God—when I'm troubled, not only in times of crisis, but in the day-to-day trials as well. It seems like the right thing to do. But I'm only human. And even more natural is my tendency to go everywhere but there.*

I also love the idea of praying—like the Bible says—without ceasing. But again, I'm all over the place. I talk to my husband, my family, my friends, and, of course, myself. I forget that the awesome Mind of God who created me—and the whole universe—can do a much better job of solving my problems than I can.

But on the darkest nights of my soul, when hopelessness consumes me, there's nowhere else to turn but God. That's when I'm brought to my knees, when I pray with all my heart. It's when I really connect. For me, crawling up into the Father's lap is a good thing because once I'm there, I realize it's where I've wanted to be all along.

Nothing is more powerful than crying, "Lord, help me." That was my plea back in the summer of 2008 when I was close to death. Occasionally His answer comes as a voice from within, sometimes as a sign. But other times it comes—seemingly out of the blue—from the mouth of a stranger.

"If you ever feel like talking . . . just buzz me down at the nurse's station."

Through teary eyes, I gaze up at Angela, one of the nurses who works the night shift at the hospital. I've gotten to know her over the last few days. She's a nice enough girl, I think, though rather young. How can she possibly understand what I'm going through? Besides, she's a nurse. She'll probably just tell me to keep doing the chemo and radiation.

I lower my head. My hands are trembling. No, I decide, I'm not sharing my heart with her.

It's hard to believe it's been only three weeks since I reluctantly started chemo and radiation. In fact, it's hard to believe I submitted to them at all. For years I studied the effects of diet and alternative methods on chronic conditions. My husband and I even co-authored a book with George Malkmus on diet and disease called The Hallelujah Diet. *My mantra has been: "If I'm ever diagnosed with cancer, I won't do chemo or radiation." Looking back, I can see I was full of unchallenged confidence. I believed a vegan diet and alternative methods would cure me. And that was that.*

Ah, the best laid plans . . .

You never know what you're going to do in a crisis situation until you're in it. My intentions were to go natural. My intuition told me to go natural. But once the doctors diagnosed, "Rectal cancer, stage III," the pressure from family and friends to take the medical route was strong. There were no guarantees on either side of the fence, but most people I knew felt the responsible choice was the insurance-covered radiation, chemotherapy, and surgery route. But my resistance was deeply ingrained, probably formed on an unconscious level starting in my first three years of life.

Soon after my birth, my mother was diagnosed with breast cancer. For much of our short time together she was either away for treatments or sick in the hospital. I recall the tension of those times in our small, hot Atlanta apartment—my mother suffering through the treatments and my father's frustration as he faced losing his wife. And I remember lying in my crib, crying every night for a year. Where was my mother?

Years later, my disillusionment with the medical protocol was further reinforced when my foster brother, Joey, was dying of cancer. I watched, this time on a very conscious level as, he too, went through painful medical treatments. I can still hear his tortured screams.

So it took a month of deliberation, before I reluctantly submitted myself to a six-week course of five-day-a-week radiation and a 24/7 chemo drip.

From the beginning, it was a disaster.

Each week, I wound up in the emergency room for some unexpected problem. Mysterious chest pains from a dislocated rib, a side effect of chemo-port surgery; sudden gushing of blood all over my clothes while in church from the malfunctioning chemo tube; and finally, on my third visit, I was admitted to the hospital with a temperature of almost 104 degrees. I became neutro-penic, a condition caused by very low red and white blood count. It makes a person vulnerable to any infection and, without medical intervention, death is almost certain. So I was put on a steady diet of blood transfusions, fluids, and heavy antibiotics.

That was three days ago.

Since then, I have been hovering between life and death. I know it sounds crazy and, just so you know, I'm not on any kind of drugs that would cause this, but ever since they wheeled me in to my room I've been haunted by what sounds like choirs of angels singing. It goes on and on, day and night. I've never heard anything like it. I've never had visions either. But every time I close my eyes I see these brilliant scenes of people—people I don't know—and they're suffering. I feel as if I'm actually leaving my body, traveling around the globe and hovering above them, feeling their pain. I've never seen anything like it. Yet even more disturbing than any of this is what takes place deep in the night. Alone, in my hospital bed, I find myself praying to die. I am so sick—every part of me is raw and out of balance—I just want out.

Each morning my oncology doctor comes by to check my progress. Always,

∞ flying high ∞

there is the unspoken question: When will the treatments start again? I, for one, can't bear to think about it. Peter can't either.

Unbeknownst to me, he is at home studying about unconventional therapies, because an inner voice is saying: 'Stowe may not survive another round of chemo and radiation.' And while Peter burns the midnight oil, poring over alternative cancer cures I sit on the edge of my bed with tears in my eyes. The words of a concerned friend echo in my head: "Be strong," she said. "You're a soldier. You have to keep going!" But I have a feeling in my gut that if I do, it will be my last battle. So I stare at the ceiling, praying for an answer. God, help me . . . What should I do?

There is a light knock on the door. Angela, the nurse, is back again. "Can I get you anything?"

I stare down at the floor and bite my lip. I feel lost—as if I am navigating through the end of my life in total darkness—not knowing where the next step is.

She moves closer, sensing my struggle. "You know . . . " *she is tentative,* "it's your body. No one knows what you're going through. And no one can make a decision about what you do with your life."

I'm surprised by her words.

"What do you really want to do?"

"I want to stop doing chemo and radiation . . . just do the alternative methods to healing . . . but it seems irresponsible. There're just no statistics to support it."

"Well, you know," *she moves closer,* "you could choose quality over quantity . . . "

I look into her soft brown eyes. It feels as if someone just opened a window and a beautiful light is streaming in. Still, I can't believe she is saying this. "But . . . you're one of them . . . Why aren't you telling me to take the medical route?"

"Look, I work here on the cancer ward. I've seen a lot of people die— sometimes horrible deaths. For some, chemo and radiation work. For others, it doesn't. But if you don't believe in it, you sure don't need to be doing it.

Follow your heart . . . do the alternatives, if you want. They may only give you a few years but you'll probably feel good for most of that time instead of being sick. You could spend it with your family . . . do whatever you like."

"But what about those who'll say I'm being irresponsible to my children?"

"What about them?" Her voice is strong and sure. "They're not the ones making this decision. You are."

I smile at Angela through teary eyes and let out a sigh, leaning back into my pillow. For the first time in a long time I feel a wave of peace wash over me. A stranger, of all people, just reminded me that this is my life—that I can live and die as I see fit.

Angela glances at her watch. "I need to make my rounds . . . I'll check back on you in a little while." She pats my foot and gives me a wink. "Sleep well."

"Angela?"

"Yes?" she turns back to me.

"Thanks."

She smiles and I see love in her eyes. "No problem."

The door closes silently behind her. I lie there, thinking about our conversation. Her message makes sense, but this isn't a decision I can make on my own so I go inward and ask for God's guidance. Help me, Lord. Tell me what do . . .

Already I'm feeling better. Tomorrow I will call Peter and tell him my decision. For now, I look out the window into the dark summer night. Here in Franklin, Tennessee, it is almost two in the morning. But somewhere in the world the sun is coming up. A sunrise . . . a new day filled with hope. Suddenly the world seems a little brighter.

carter's court

*For true success ask yourself these four questions:
Why? Why not? Why not me? Why not now?*

—JAMES ALLEN

I t was the early 1970's and Calvin's life was in high gear. With a
successful construction company under his belt, he began dreaming
of how he could be of service to his hometown community—Franklin.
Since the inception of the Interstate Highway System in 1956, small
towns all over America were dying. Franklin was no exception. Calvin
was troubled to see the traffic that once frequented his small community routed away to national chain stores in shopping malls. He had an
idea how to bring them back.

This concern for his community launched one of the biggest and
most difficult projects of his life. It was also the venture that helped
crystallize the largest shift in Calvin's thinking. He named it Carter's
Court, after the historic Carter House—a Civil War landmark—across
the street from his property. Everything about it was unique—the
location, the design, the financing, and the construction. What began
as an unusual shopping center ended up as one of Tennessee's largest
tourist attractions.

Peter and I drove by it for years, and now that we realized it was Calvin's creation, we wondered how it came to be. Calvin's response was typical.

"Low IQ, I guess." He laughed and took a sip of his coffee.

I gave him my best evil eye. "I don't buy that . . . "

"Actually, I got the idea years ago when I was in the National Guard. We visited Europe and it was so beautiful there—the little cobblestone streets, the baker living above the bakery shop, and the balconies in the small stores along the street. I just fell in love with it. I could see it so clearly—a quaint little European village. That was the picture in my mind!"

Calvin pointed toward the wall to a framed, faded clipping from *Southern Living* magazine dated November 1976. I read the headline out loud, "A European Village with a Southern Flair."

"Back then I was president of the Chamber of Commerce, and for the longest time I'd been trying to convince the shop owners downtown that if we had sidewalk cafes, antique stores, and specialty shops we'd be able to draw people away from the mall and back into Franklin. But it fell on deaf ears."

"They weren't ready for it?"

"No, but this was around the time I was getting all fired up about the Science of Mind principles. I'd already bought a piece of land downtown, and one Sunday morning something just clicked in my mind—a divine inspiration. I thought, *I'll build my own little village. I'll show them it'll work.*" Calvin leaned back and let out a sigh. "I didn't know it then, but the odds were against me."

"Why?"

"First of all," he straightened and held up three fingers, "in real estate we're taught that the three most important things above all are: location, location, location. I didn't even have one of those things. The land I'd purchased . . . well, it really was not on the best side of town.

"Down the street a friend of mine was also starting a development, only he'd bought a $1 million block on the square. Plus, he'd hired a New York consultant *and* an architect from California. And here I was, starting the foundation and the framing and I hadn't even inquired about the financing!"

Calvin squared his shoulders for a perfect Forrest Gump imitation. "You see. That's dumb! But I'd already put my foot out there—I couldn't back up. Anyway, I'd have probably quit if I'd applied for the financing first 'cause that's when I found out they don't make loans for people who do silly things like that!"

The goofy expression on Calvin's face made me laugh.

"Yeah, it's easy to joke about now, but I sure wasn't laughing then. I found out that in specialty shops like this you've got to have a tremendous volume of people coming in. You need to be next to a big resort or an interstate, or have a population of at least 300,000 . . . You know what Franklin's population was?"

I shook my head.

"Only 17,000 people . . . and it was *eighteen* miles away from Nashville! I heard the same thing from every bank and insurance company I talked to: 'Calvin, nobody in his right mind is going to drive twenty miles to come to your little development.' The sad thing was that I almost started to believe them."

"Were you tempted to give up?" I was sure that's what I would've done in his place.

"Yes, but I still had all these principles running through my mind, only I didn't realize I was using them in a *negative* way. I was starting to believe the people who were saying, 'This won't work, fella.' I began to think, *Maybe they're right.* And all of a sudden, I could *see* the negatives.

"For instance, there weren't any magnet stores to draw shoppers to the area—no K-mart, no Sears. There wasn't even a movie theater . . . " He let out a sigh. "Still, that didn't bother me so much."

"But you needed to draw people in."

"Yes, I know. I thought about that all the time. And one day something clicked." Calvin snapped his fingers. "I thought, *A restaurant! That'll draw people!*"

"Ah," I nodded.

"Maybe it was a coincidence, but I just *happened* to meet this wonderful couple with a great reputation. They'd never been in the restaurant business, but they had a fantastic barbecue recipe. So I talked them into coming on board.

"Financing was probably my biggest challenge. No local bank was interested in my old-world village idea—back then everyone was into new and modern-type malls. Five banks turned me down . . ."

I shook my head, amazed at his perseverance.

"That's when I realized I'd have to go out of state. I went clear up to Richmond, Virginia, gave them my pitch and, I think, because they were close to Williamsburg they could identify with the old-timey buildings and how they attract tourists."

"And Carter's Court . . ." I said. "Isn't that an historic area where the Battle of Franklin was fought?"

"Right. I called it Carter's Court because a family by the name of Carter had originally owned the land, and their house was already a landmark . . .

"So the bank in Richmond agreed to loan me half of the money, if I could get 80 percent of my tenants signed up and have the development finished by a certain date. And, by the way," Calvin sighed, "this was all going on in the middle of a recession—"

"Oh . . ."

"I thought, *That's impossible.* It just felt like everything was against me. I'd come home every night feeling so down and I'd partake of that good old Tennessee product—Jack Daniels. Now, Marilyn wasn't too happy about that, and to tell the truth, I didn't know what to do or who to talk to. Downtown, people were literally taking bets on whose development was going to make it . . . and I don't know of anyone who was betting on me."

"It sounds so stressful . . . "

"Well, it was. But I owned some timberland a few miles away and I found that just going out there and walking in the woods became my greatest escape. Being in nature, sitting on a log, and just relaxing really helped me . . . gave me a different perspective on the situation. After a while, I came to a very positive conclusion—I had nowhere to go but up.

"To make it work, I knew I had to start thinking positively. So I began *visualizing* tenants coming in. And to this day, I still get chill bumps just thinking about how they came to me from out of the blue. And, by the way, they ended up being mostly women who had never been in business before."

"No business experience? That seems risky."

"Maybe it was, Stowe. But I had a gut feeling that was the way to go . . . so I just went with it. We took an old two-story house, put wheels on it, and moved it back where we were building. Then I put my desk in there and started playing the role of executive. I pictured them coming to me and when they did, I took their applications . . . gladly.

"Before long we had every space filled. But I still needed another restaurant. So along came a lady named Daisy. I remember the day she came to interview. 'Daisy . . . ' I got my pen and paper ready. 'How much experience do you have in the restaurant business?'

"'Well,' she smiled sweetly, 'my friend here, Linda, and I, have made some blueberry muffins and tarts and we've sold them to the Civic Club.'

"I stared at her and swallowed hard. 'Anything else?'

"'Why, no,' She continued smiling.

"But I wasn't smiling. I thought *Oh, no!* I almost slid under the table. This was a little out there, even for me. But Daisy, bless her heart, stood tall and said something that really struck close to home."

"'Mr. LeHew, I am going to treat *every* person that comes into my restaurant like they're friends in my home.'

"She had such *confidence*. And I'll tell you, that meant something to me, though later on it would prove to be a problem. You see, Daisy didn't want to *charge* people. I guess she really meant it . . . they were all her friends!

"So when Daisy's partner, Linda pulled out, Marilyn and I decided to become silent partners in Miss Daisy's Tea Room. We opened up our first restaurant with used kitchen equipment for $6,000."

"I've always heard that's a tough business to make a profit in."

"You heard right . . . in fact, it's terrible. It wears you down in so many ways. You have to keep your eye on the goal continuously and try to see past the problems, of which we had plenty. But even though we were working on a tight budget and serving folks out of an old house, Miss Daisy's was an overnight success. And it was doing just what I wanted it to—bringing people into Carter's Court."

"So did Miss Daisy's bring in all the traffic you wanted?"

"It definitely helped. But we needed more . . . and fast. A local bank had loaned me the other half of the construction costs on a temporary ninety-day note, and I'll be honest with you, my back was up against the wall . . . "

Calvin pressed his lips together and tapped his fingers lightly on the desk. "For a while there, I wasn't sure if we would make it."

a click
of an idea

*You attract to you the things you expect,
think about, and hold in your mind.*

—FROM CALVIN'S *MANIFESTING DREAMS*

Calvin LeHew set his goals, stayed true to his vision, and built a
one-of-a-kind shopping center. Despite all the setbacks, he faithfully pursued this dream, hoping to inspire other businesses downtown
to follow his lead. He also hoped that if he built it, people would come.
But, observing the nearly deserted sidewalks of Carter's Court one day,
Calvin had to admit—he had a bad situation—not enough traffic to support his new development.

He could have panicked. Instead, a quote by Ernest Holmes inspired him. "Every problem contains its own answer if you think of
the problem merely as a question, an inquiry, and not as an obstruc-
tion. Thinking of it this way, keep your mind not on the repetition of
thoughts about the problem, but on the receipt of a definite answer."

"So I thought, Where is *the traffic?*" Calvin held up a finger. "The
answer was: *Out by the interstate.* My first idea was a billboard." Calvin
shook his head. "Too expensive. Then I thought of putting a TV with advertising in the hotel lobbies, but I realized after a while that the clerks

would probably get bored and switch channels.

"I kept my mind open, though, waiting for the answer. One day, while visiting one of our shops, I saw something interesting—a Sony BetaMax video player with a wire running to a TV and a video explaining how to make oriental rugs." Calvin tapped his right temple. "Something just *clicked* in my mind. I thought, *I could run a wire from a video player to all the TV sets in a motel and tell about Carter's Court.*

"Serendipitously, there was a fellow in the shop next door who knew about video and was willing to help us. Next, I talked to a motel owner out by the interstate, and asked if we could experiment with this. He agreed and we ran our video feed on a vacant channel. We named it *TourAd.* The housekeeping staff was instructed to leave the TVs on the *TourAd* channel to welcome the new guests."

"How'd it work?"

"There were a few problems, but one by one we figured them out. First, the *TourAd* channel bled over into the other channels, so we fixed that. Then the BetaMax player overheated in the linen closet where it was stored. We put in a fan to cool it. Then lint got into the video player, so we had to install a filter. It shows that you're going to run into obstacles, but you don't have to let them defeat you. There's always an answer.

"Did it bring people into Carter's Court?"

"Yes, but that wasn't all. We'd created a new business—selling advertising in hotels! We started with some local antique dealers but eventually we were selling ads and full productions to the City of Nashville. They used it to advertise their own tourist spots, like the Parthenon. At one time, *TourAd* was airing in 5,000 hotel rooms in Nashville. And here I was again, like with the drugstores, in a business I knew nothing about . . . so I sold it for a profit and concentrated on our booming business at Carter's Court.

"Sounds like a win-win to me . . . "

"It was," he said. "And I had another similar situation happen at Miss Daisy's . . . "

I nodded, encouraging him to go on.

"Well, like I said before, Miss Daisy's was doing well. Why, we had people *lined up* to eat there. And afterwards, these same folks were shopping at our other twenty-four stores—they were paying my rent. Still, the restaurant itself wasn't making much money and somewhere in my mind, I was searching for a way to change that.

"Every day I'd come down and work the cash register. I enjoyed taking the money and talking to customers. Every day I heard the same questions: 'Would you share your cream chicken recipe?' Or, 'I'd love to know how to make Miss Daisy's beef casserole.' After a while, I became aware of a unique *possibility.*

"Finally, one day, it *clicked.* I immediately went back into the kitchen: 'Miss Daisy, Marilyn, we're going to have to put out a cookbook!' They got right on it, putting together the recipes. Then I took them down to a local fellow who had a printing press in the back of his house."

"No publisher?"

"Nope, I didn't know any better, and because of this we saved a lot of money. Over the years Miss Daisy's cookbook has sold over a million copies. Just out of that one little *click* of an idea, we've made more money than several restaurants . . . we're still getting royalties from it." He turned in his chair and rolled over to the bookshelf. "Let's see . . . " His hand waved back and forth over the books. "Ah, here it is."

He handed me a copy of *Miss Daisy's Cookbook.* We were quiet for a moment as I flipped through pages of appetizing southern recipes. They looked delicious. But now, hearing Calvin's story, they seemed like more than just recipes; they were food for thought—that keeping an open mind and acting upon those little inspired ideas can pay off.

I put the book back on Calvin's desk. He raised his hand. "Keep it."

"Thanks."

"I learned a lot from that book . . . and the *TourAd* channel. The biggest lesson is not to think so much about the problem, but to keep an open mind and believe that the answers will come. And more often than not, things turn out better than you ever imagined."

"Say, that reminds me of another story . . . an answered prayer, actually." Calvin leaned in, putting his elbows on the desk. "It was around that same time, and I was financially overextended . . . way overextended."

"Uh, oh. What happened?"

"I'd been aggressively borrowing money, buying farms and timberland and such. One day a bank official called me into his office. He said, 'Calvin, you've only been paying interest on your loans and, well . . . it's time to pay up on the principle. We need $350,000—within two weeks. If you can't come up with it, we'll either have an auction, or foreclose on your properties.'

Calvin rubbed the back of his neck. "This probably ranks up there as the second worst day in my life. Marilyn and I were about to lose everything we'd worked for. We needed to sell some real estate in a hurry. But we were in the middle of a recession. So I prayed for a miracle.

"I didn't know it at that moment, but one was on the way. Later that night I got a call from Tom T. Hall, the songwriter of 'Harper Valley PTA,' and a lot of other hits. He and his wife, Dixie, were good friends and we'd worked together on projects for homeless animals. Tom said, 'I've just come into some money, and I would like to buy some land to build a cabin where I can write songs. I wonder if you know of any neighbors out your way that might want to sell?' "

Calvin lowered his voice. "I said, 'Tom . . . I'll be honest with you, I'm in financial difficulty right now and if you'll meet me tomorrow out at my farm, I'll make you a deal you can't refuse!' "

"So we met the next day. I'd already divided the property up into tracts a few months earlier but I hadn't sold any, so they were still intact. I gave Tom the plat and we began surveying the long hollow. He didn't say a word, but just kept writing things down. My heart was about to beat out of my chest.

"Finally, Tom spoke. 'Okay,' he announced, 'I'll take tracks one, two, three, and four.' Then he added it up." Calvin let out a deep sigh. "Stowe, it came to $350,000—exactly what we needed. I was about to cry. I just closed my eyes. 'Thank you, God, Jesus . . . everybody!' What started as one of the worst days of my life, turned into one of the happiest.

"'It's a deal.' I reached out to shake on it.

"Then Tom suddenly asked, 'What's today's date?'

"'Well, let's see . . . it's Thursday the twelfth. Why?'

"Tom replied, 'Dixie and I got married on Friday the thirteenth, and I wrote my best song on Friday the thirteenth. So we've got to close *tomorrow!*'"

"Well, by then I was just vibrating with enthusiasm—I could move mountains! I immediately began attempting the impossible, getting a title ready in one day instead of the usual two weeks. I was ready to pay armed guards and lawyers to work all night long."

Thankfully, Calvin did not have to do that. With the help of his attorney, Jack Robinson, he and Marilyn were able to meet Tom and Dixie at the bank the next day with a cashier's check, which was then put into escrow. They had a formal signing of the contract on Friday the thirteenth—just as Tom had wished—and let the attorneys work it out later. Everyone was happy—especially Calvin. It was another answer to prayer, for which Calvin has never ceased to be thankful.

a friend
of calvin's

In my friend, I find a second self.

—Isabel Norton

I stared at the caller ID on my cell phone. *Calvin?* It was almost 6:30 pm. *Why is he calling at this hour?* Calvin is an early-to-bed, early-to-rise kind of man, usually hitting the sack not long after dinner. *He must have something on his mind.* I picked up the phone.

"Mr. LeHew . . . to what do I owe this honor?"

"I was just headed off to bed but I wanted to let you know about a good friend of mine—a kindred spirit—who's coming into town tomorrow night. Her name's Rita Davenport. I met her back when I had Carter's Court . . . a friend of Miss Daisy's. Back then, she had her own TV talk show . . . talked to anybody who was anybody. Since then she's been a very popular motivational speaker."

"Sounds like someone I'd like to meet."

"You know, I really think you'd enjoy her. Remember how we were talking about hearing all those negative voices growing up?"

"Mm hm . . ."

"Well, Rita heard quite a few herself . . . but she didn't let them hold her back. Her whole life has been so inspiring, a real rags to riches story. She's had a big influence on me . . . Anyway, these days she's the head of an international cosmetics company. She travels quite a bit doing speaking engagements."

"Is that why she's coming to town?"

"Yep, she's speaking at Lowe's Vanderbilt Plaza tomorrow night for a few thousand of her associates . . . and she wants me to open for her. Thought you and Peter might want to come."

"Sure, we'd love to!"

The hotel convention center was crowded. Standing room only. Calvin just stepped off the stage after giving a well-received and shortened version of his life story, and now the woman of the hour was taking the spotlight. Rita Davenport. My eyes followed the well-lit dynamo across the room as she paced back and forth on the stage. Rita painted word pictures like a seasoned humorist, mixing her life story with homespun wisdom and dancing through everything from funny childhood memories, to a new line of skin conditioners, to the latest headlines. She has what every gifted motivational speaker has—the ability to make you feel like she's speaking just to you.

"My friends, we are tested constantly. And with every adversity in life there is a gift. But it's up to us to find that gift. Sometimes it takes a little detective work. As it happens we learn more from adversity than we do from success. I always like to remember that I'm being challenged and tested. And I hope I pass this test and learn what I need to, so I don't have to do it over again. I have to laugh because sometimes I think God has more optimism about me than I have about myself, or He wouldn't put me through some of these things.

"But this, too, shall pass . . . for we know that life is cyclical—our health, our work, and our relationships—they're constantly changing. We have to realize that sometimes a setback is just a *setup* for a *comeback*. *Believe* in yourself and *be* yourself! I always say be yourself because everyone else is taken.

"It's important to realize that we have so much going for us that we take many things for granted. Each one of us is gifted in some way. It might be cooking, speaking, mathematics . . . or maybe you're a singer, writer, or painter. We all have talent. And God has sent us here with a purpose. He's given us an assignment along with all the necessary talent to fulfill that purpose. Sometimes it's a struggle, but it's up to us to polish our skills to become good enough to use that talent."

Rita definitely had my attention. Her reminder of the need to nurture our individuality, to dig down deep within ourselves and find the courage to risk stepping out was timely . . . and encouraging. I loved her openness and honesty, how she shared her life story with us so transparently.

"As a child, I had a speech impediment and in first grade the school labeled me as having a learning disability—they were going to put me in a special education class. About that time my mother took me to California to visit her sick sister. While we were there she had the California school system test me. Afterwards, they called to give her the results. Mother was sure the news would be bad. 'I think I know what you're going to say . . . Rita has problems.'

"'No,' they said. 'She's gifted! We suggest she be moved to the third grade.' Funny . . . in Tennessee, they thought I had a learning disability but in California I was 'gifted.' When I got back home I walked into my first grade class and announced, 'Miss Tyler, guess what? I'm going to help you with the other students!' I believed I was smart and I *expected* to be treated that way. If I had ended up in special education classes, I might not be where I am today."

Rita zeroed right in on what I needed to be reminded of . . . it was a message I could never hear enough. I guess that was why I liked hanging around positive people like Rita's friend, Calvin.

"We all need people to motivate and inspire us," she continued. "But we don't always have that. So what do we do? We have to read books, listen to CDs, and go to training. I love reading biographies of people whom I admire—it's inspiring. It helps expand your mind and eliminate the negatives. Every minute you spend with a negative thought takes a hundred minutes to erase it. We have to replace those negative things that have been told to us, sometimes innocently as children. And remember, people treat you the way they feel about themselves. If someone is not treating you well, you've got to get away if you can, and be around people that can motivate you—folks that are fun, excited, and on purpose.

"And then go out and be that kind of person for someone else. Motivate others to learn and love—these are two very important things to do in life. And just be nicer than necessary because it will always come back to you. My daddy set the example that *what goes around comes around*. He was a mechanic. And it seemed to me that he helped every motorist with car trouble.

"I used to ask him, 'Daddy, do you have to help everybody?'

"And he'd say, 'Yes, I do, Rita, 'cause some day you might be stranded out on the highway and somebody is going to help you because I'm helping this guy right now.'

"Now I've been out on a highway before with car trouble . . . and the people my daddy helped weren't anywhere around—but guess what? Somebody else stopped. I always say, 'Thank you, Daddy.' Because, truly, what goes around comes around.

"Find ways to do things for other people that don't benefit you. You'll be rewarded somehow, somewhere along the way.

"And be grateful for what you have. The first mental adjustment for prosperity is gratitude—appreciating what you have right now, no matter how humble. If you have a place to sleep tonight . . . food to eat, and a family around you . . . be thankful for them. Those things are so important. It helps to make a list of all the things you're grateful for.

Rita surveyed the room, taking the pulse of her audience. "We all have stress in our lives," she continued. "Whenever I feel anxious, I ask myself, *Is this really the worst thing that can happen to me?* I usually reflect, well, the worst thing would be for something to happen to my husband. Then next, my children, and my family members—or my house could burn down . . . I actually had that happen!

"God definitely works in mysterious ways because I had really been wanting a new house. But my husband didn't want to move. Well, as it happened, lightning struck and burned our house down—a total loss. So we had to build it back. See, it all worked out perfectly—I got a new house and he didn't have to move!" Rita stood there, smiling as the audience erupted into laughter. "Now, you think about it. It was an act of God and I simply appreciated it. But back when I was going through all the cleanup of the fire I wondered, *Do I really need to go through this?*"

For forty minutes, I was mesmerized by this charming and inspiring woman. Now, sitting in the back, I watched her pause and catch her breath. I had a feeling she was winding down.

" . . . Nothing's better to me than the story of Captain Sullenberger and Flight 1549 . . . " The audience burst into applause. It had been only a few months since the heroic airline pilot safely landed a disabled US Airways Airbus carrying 155 people in the Hudson River. " . . . He said something important to his crew and passengers just before the plane hit the water. You know what he told them?" Rita's voice trembled. "Now I get emotional . . . because I want you to always remember his words—'Brace for impact.' He warned his passengers and crew to brace themselves . . . to *prepare* for impact.

"My friends, you don't know what's ahead of you . . . you don't know. Prepare for impact right now so your children can benefit from all of your efforts, both while you're here, and after you're gone. *Prepare for impact.* That's my assignment to you." With these words Rita threw up her hand to the audience. "I love you all! Good-night!"

rita speaks to my heart

If you don't change your beliefs,
your life will be like this forever. Is that good news?

—ROBERT ANTONY

Calvin introduced us to Rita after the event. She was very receptive to Peter's invitation for an interview the following day at Calvin and Marilyn's home.

Early the next morning, Peter and the crew set up the camera and lights in the LeHew's living room while I jotted down a few questions for Rita. Calvin told me she'd been raised with a lot of negative voices and I hoped to learn how she overcame them. I had butterflies in my stomach so I took a deep breath and glanced up from my notes. Standing off to the side, I watched as Rita talked with Calvin—she appeared confident, friendly, and most all, accessible. I had a feeling this would be a good interview.

Soon Peter had the lighting and sound set up. Rita and I took our places, locked eyes, and started at the beginning.

"Okay," I cleared my throat. "Could you tell me about your childhood?"

Rita relaxed into her chair. "When I reflect on my background now, I feel very grateful . . . though at the time I was self-conscious about my circumstances. You see, I was raised in poverty in a little area called Flat Rock, Tennessee. We didn't have indoor plumbing and I was ashamed of my house, my situation, and my clothes. Things like positive influences and encouragement were scarce. I can still hear those voices of long ago . . .

"'Don't try and get above your raisin', Rita. Nobody in this family ever had anything or graduated from high school. So don't go havin' high hopes . . .'

"Hearing that I couldn't help but wonder, *Well, what good are low hopes?* I just didn't see life the way they did. I might've been a little thing but I had big dreams. I stood right up and told 'em what I wanted out of life. 'Someday, I'm going to go to college. I'm going to have a nice car and pretty clothes. And I'm going to have a home that'll make Scarlet O'Hara's Tara look like a tract house.'"

This struck me as a bold statement. "Where did that kind of spunk and attitude come from?"

"I don't know, Stowe . . . I was an oddity in my family. I guess I was just born with determination and optimism. I had big dreams. I wanted nice things. I wanted to travel. And even though I could see the negatives around me I realized they were temporary. Somehow, I knew it was just a learning experience I had to go through—that someday I would have more, be more, learn more, and earn more so that eventually I could share more.

"Oh, they teased me and made fun of me but I didn't let it stop me. I stayed focused on what I wanted. Some people just have that natural persistence and confidence—it doesn't matter what their surroundings are. Look at Dolly Parton. She's a great example of someone who overcame severe poverty. And it's because she looked *beyond* her circumstances. She saw the possibilities.

"Unfortunately, my older sister got married at fourteen. She didn't even finish the ninth grade. So I didn't have an example of someone striving for a higher education. When I finally got to high school I was discouraged at every turn. I'll never forget a conversation with my high school counselor . . .

"'Ms. Clemmons, when I go to college I'm going to—'

"'Look here, Rita. I don't mean to dash your dreams . . . but, honey, you're just *not* college material. You're sweet . . . and you're right personable, but the best you can do is find some nice boy and get married. Have a family, but don't waste your time dreaming about going to college.'

"Now that hurt. But, again, I didn't let it get me down. I wanted to be a leader. Why, I remember in sixth grade organizing my class to do something special for the school . . . turned out to be very successful. Later, I was in the student government. From the beginning, I had high expectations.

"In my career, I've done a lot of things; TV talk show host, motivational speaker, and of course, I've been a businesswoman. Back then, I didn't know about any of that. So in high school, I focused on home economics . . . "

"Home economics?" That surprised me. "Coming from someone like you, that's hard to believe."

"Well, you have to remember . . . I didn't know a soul who was going to college and I figured those would be skills I could use someday when I got married and had a family. After I graduated, I got a job in an insurance company. I worked hard, saving my money for something I really wanted—a Corvette. I could just see myself behind the wheel."

She could *see herself behind the wheel.* Rita, like her friend Calvin, used the power of visualization to bring about what she wanted in life.

"There was no doubt," Rita continued, "that if I had a Corvette I'd get a lot of attention. But one day it hit me: *If I get a car that fancy, I'm gonna need some nice clothes.* And then I realized I couldn't park it in front of our house. I mean, we didn't even have indoor plumbing . . . it would've looked tacky."

"So what'd you do?"

"I did what was right for me. I invested in myself. I *had* to get an education and that meant college. And even though I'd been told I wasn't college material, I graduated from Middle Tennessee State University in three years *with honors*. Every semester, even though money was tight, I paid two dollars to have a copy of my grades sent to my high school counselor. I thought she deserved to know that although she might've had doubts about me, I certainly didn't.

"Later, when the university honored me as a distinguished alumni I invited her to have lunch with the president of the University and be part of the celebration. And when they asked me to speak at the university's commencement in front of 16,000 people I invited her again to be my special guest."

"By now, I guess she believed in you . . . "

"I think so . . . and I share this as an example . . . when folks tell you that you can't or you shouldn't do things, it can be fuel for ambition. We always have a choice—to shut down or fire up. I chose to fire up. I wasn't going to let someone else determine what I could do with my life."

Rita paused, her eyes narrowing into a wise, thoughtful gaze. It felt like she was reading my mind because from the moment we'd met she had been speaking to my heart. *When we dare to dream, pursue our purpose and share our unique gifts, we will hit resistance. It may appear as fear, doubt, distracting mind-chatter or self-criticism. Forget those negative voices—don't let them hold you back from doing what you were born to do.* In the span of less than twenty-four hours her message rang loud and clear: Don't listen to the naysayers. Listen to your heart.

april 27, 2009

*M*EETING WITH CALVIN *these last few months is beginning to have a positive effect on me. I see it in the little things. Setting goals is giving me direction. Reading inspiring books is giving me encouragement— my body can be healed. And being conscientious about what I say and think is making me feel better about myself.*

In addition to all that, I'm also spending more time being still. And, as so often happens when things are quiet, you hear things you've never heard before. From somewhere deep inside, I hear my internal alarm clock ringing. Suddenly, my eyes are open and there is an incredible realization—I've been hitting the snooze bar for much too long—it's time to wake up.

The mid-life wakeup call—especially coupled with a life-threatening disease—requires action. And wisdom. So I seek the counsel of family, friends, and those who have the gift of healing.

One day, I visit Mary Glesige, a woman I met through Calvin. She practices Reiki, a Japanese technique for stress reduction that also promotes healing. Spiritually-guided practitioners, like Mary, hold their hands above a person and serve as a conduit for healing energy. I have done it several times and find it very relaxing.

After our session we chat for a few minutes. "So, Stowe . . . " Mary's eyes twinkle. "When's the last time you did anything creative? Just something you like to do for you?"

"Hmm . . . " I shrug my shoulders. "It's been a while." I think back over the last few years—our lives have been so busy. With homeschooling, work, and taking care of the children and the house, my favorite creative outlet— songwriting—has fallen by the wayside.

Mary leans in close. "I want to suggest you go home today and make something, write something . . . whatever it is that makes your heart happy. Okay? Can you do that?"

"Alright . . . maybe I'll write a song. I haven't done that in a while."

Inspired, a song comes to me on the way home. A few days later, I find myself writing another one. Before long, I'm back in the songwriting saddle— doing what I was born to do. I feel excited, alive. I am connected again to God's music. And the very best part is that, unlike when I was in the music business, I feel free to write any kind of song my heart desires.

What a revelation. I am free!

Freedom . . . a given in this wonderful land of opportunity. Yet, I often feel bound by unseen shackles—voices from the past, outdated ways of approaching life and, the most constricting fetter of all—FEAR (I remember Calvin telling me the acronym for FEAR: False Evidence Appearing Real). By moving beyond my fear I am free to live the full range of possibilities that God, in His infinite mercy offers me.

We are each unique in our talents, possessing the ability to do something that no one else on earth can do. I know this in my head. So why, then, do I hold back? Why do I put mundane jobs or gathering earthly treasures, ahead of that burning desire flowing from deep within? I don't know about everyone else, but for me it's fear—fear that I might fail, that I might not be good enough. Or maybe it's a fear that I might succeed beyond my wildest dreams, and then would have to face all the responsibilities that go with it.

Fortunately, I've gotten a wake-up call. I refer to it as the gift of cancer. Cancer has given me the chance to slow down, to focus on more of what's important. Not everyone is so lucky. Some die suddenly, taking their dreams with them. Others just live in fear or denial of who they are meant to be.

I don't know how long I'm going to live, but I do know one thing; I don't want to die with the music still in me. I cannot let the fear of failure, or success, keep me from being comfortable in my skin. I begin to realize, I don't have to go out and re-create myself, God has already done that. All I have to do is allow His Light to shine through me—to be who I was meant to be.

With that in mind, I am inspired one morning to write a song. I call it Wake Up. It is an up tempo, thought-provoking song, tailor made to rouse me from my fearful imaginings. Singing it alone in my bedroom, it feels personal, like a gift just for me. But once I begin performing it in public, it becomes a gift for others as well.

Wake Up

Stop the clock from ringin'
Hit the floor the door it's rainin'
Ah it's just another day
Another day

Get to work and hurry
If you can't play or pray don't worry
'Cause there'll be another day
Will there be another day

Chorus:
Wake up Wake up Wake up
Don't you see that you're asleep
Wake up Wake up Wake up
And be who you were meant to be

Reflect in the mirror
Is the future any clearer
Or have you just closed your eyes
Just close your eyes

And hear the voice inside you
Still the will and let it guide you
Oh you know it's not too late
Oh it's not too late

(Chorus)

Beyond the water-colored blue
Across the river someone's calling you

(Chorus)

You were meant to be (2x)
Be who you were meant to be

chapter 25

is that all there is?

*Ego has a voracious appetite,
the more you feed it, the hungrier it gets.*

—NATHANIEL BRONNER JR.

We were well into the Tennessee spring, past the daffodils and forsythia, but still enjoying the redbuds and dogwoods. At The Factory, our Monday morning meetings had also developed into something Peter and I took pleasure in. We really liked Calvin's positive attitude—it was always there—even in the little things. For instance, my "How ya doing?" was often answered with "good, and gettin' better." Not a brag, just optimistic self-talk. No matter what was going on, he liked to keep his words upbeat.

I pulled out my laptop to check my notes about Carter's Court. "Let's pick up where . . . you had finally seen success after struggling for so long."

"Yes," He rubbed his chin. "Launching Carter's Court was a difficult undertaking for me, but now it was thriving. I was feeling successful, and . . . " A smile crept across his face. "I was looking good in the community!"

"Ahh."

"Suddenly, I was the bank's golden boy. They liked what I was doing. So they made me a bank director. Then they made me an executive bank director! Here I was, one of three people making all the major decisions for the biggest and oldest bank in Williamson County."

"You were on a roll."

"I'll say . . . I became president of the Chamber of Commerce, then chairman of the Zoning Board. I was chairman of the Housing Authority, and on and on. I was Man of the Year! I had my picture on the front page of the paper almost every week. But after a while, it started getting embarrassing. I was on fourteen boards of directorship—civic, social, and business—and it felt like all these responsibilities were taking over my life. I was doing nothing but going to meetings . . . "

I shook my head. It all sounded like torture to me.

"Talk about ego getting in the way—I was on a crash course. I'd become so full of myself, I thought I could do almost anything. One day I got an emergency call at my office at Carter's Court. The jewelry store had just been robbed. Without thinking, I went down to see what I could do.

"As soon as I got there, I saw a guy running across the parking lot. He had a gun and a pillowcase full of stuff, which I assumed was the jewelry. I couldn't catch him by foot so I jumped into my pickup truck and, slinging gravel and making a lot of noise, started out after him. I turned down one road, but I didn't see anyone. So I went to the only other street where he could be. There was a young man walking casually along . . . but no bag or gun.

"I panicked. *Is that him?* I knew I had to make a quick decision: Do I go up to him, and ask, 'Mister, did you just rob Melba's jewelry store?' Or do I just tackle him, throw him to the ground, and ask forgiveness later if he's *not* the robber? I decided on the latter.

I stifled a laugh. What a predicament.

"Now I've seen lots of Roy Rogers movies—he was one of my favorite stars along with his horse, Trigger—so I knew what to do."

"Oh, no . . . " I could see where this was going.

Calvin's hands gripped an imaginary steering wheel. "With my truck still running, I pulled up next to him, opened the door, and jumped out right on top of him. He was a big fellow, but I grabbed him and threw him to the ground. He hit the road with a thud. And in that very tense moment, when I wondered if I'd made a mistake, he said the most beautiful words—like music to my ears." Calvin held up both hands as if he were surrendering. "'Please, Mister . . . ' he said, 'let me go! I've never done anything like this before.' He admitted his guilt right there to me. Boy, was I relieved.

"Of course, I didn't let him go. One of my employees helped me hold him down until police came. I found out later that when he'd heard my truck coming, he threw the jewelry and the gun over a fence into a neighbor's yard. So afterwards, I did a little sleuthing and retrieved the pillowcase, along with the gun.

Calvin took a deep breath. "I guess I was programmed from an early age to play the part of the hero—jumping off horses onto villains— the good guy fighting crime. So, that was my self-image. It felt good to impress the police and be written up in the newspaper. Oh . . . the Chamber of Commerce awarded me a plaque with a pair of shackles. The caption read, 'Next time use handcuffs.' That became a big joke.

"All of this was quite a big boost to my ego and, for a while there, life was definitely good; I couldn't lose. Then one day, I got out my financial statements . . . just running the numbers, when I suddenly realized I'd reached my goal. I couldn't believe it. I was a *millionaire*—at age thirty-three—*two years* ahead of schedule!"

"You must have been on top of the world!"

"Nope . . . " he frowned, "just the opposite."

"I don't know what I was expecting. Maybe I thought trumpets would sound: *You did it!* Instead, I felt kind of sad. I'd finally reached my goal, but my life was empty. My purpose was gone. It's a theory of mine that folks like Elvis Presley, Judy Garland, and Marilyn

Monroe started out with big goals. And I imagine that when they finally reached them, they found themselves asking, *Is this all there is?* Maybe that's why they drank or took drugs . . . or committed suicide. There was nothing left for them to conquer.

"I know that's the way I felt that day. I remembered that Peggy Lee song, *Is That All There Is?* Here, I'd worked so hard . . . and I finally got it, only to discover *that ain't it.* Fame and fortune, they're not what life's about. I felt lost . . . I didn't know what I was looking for anymore."

"What did you do?"

"Something deep inside led me back to the woods. I spent a lot of time alone . . . just praying and thinking. I read books that spoke to my heart and it came to me that I'd let my life become very imbalanced. I began to see an analogy of a tripod with three legs—spiritual, physical, and mental. It's so important to keep each leg balanced with the others. But I hadn't done that. I'd let my ego get too big.

"But during this quiet time, that changed. I don't know when it happened exactly, but there was a peaceful feeling that slowly came to me. My life started to come into balance.

"I finally understood that fame and material things are not what life's about. At the same time, I was also coming to a realization about the principles I'd been studying—*This stuff really works!* Proverbs 23:7 says, 'For as [a man] thinketh *in his heart,* so is he.' I was keenly aware that what a man holds in his heart, or thinks, has a great effect upon him—physically, mentally, and spiritually. From out of my very thoughts I'd been able to build things out of nothing . . . against great odds. I sensed there was a greater purpose for my life, although I didn't yet know what that was. I was just beginning to see that I could do even *greater* works that would benefit others using these same techniques. All of this fascinated me. I was hungry to learn more."

"One day I told Marilyn I wanted to go to The Church Of Religious Science headquarters . . . out in Los Angeles. I wanted to study these principles."

Although today I see him as a teacher, I can also see that Calvin has always been an enthusiastic student. Even now, when there are questions, Calvin goes in search of answers. So I wasn't surprised he was willing to move out of his comfort zone and relocate to California to continue his studies. For him it was a natural tack, navigating toward his destination. But what about Marilyn? How do you ask your wife to uproot her life?

Calvin shook his head. "She wasn't too keen on it to begin with. We went round and round . . . and it almost broke us up."

"Really?"

He nodded slowly. "I finally told her, 'Marilyn, I'm going with or without you.'"

I sat back in my seat. What an ultimatum. And it's a testament to their marriage . . . they are still together.

california dreaming

*Don't be afraid to listen to your own inner urgings
to be creative . . . to walk away from the crowd.
That's the only way you can truly risk and grow.*

—From Calvin's *Manifesting Dreams*

We'd been talking for a while when a large stack of mail suddenly appeared in the small window-like opening between the offices of Calvin and his accountant. He placed the pile on his desk and sorted through the envelopes. "Bill . . . bill . . . hmm, what's this? Oh, it's an invitation to a retreat . . . bill, bill . . . Okay. Enough of that." He moved the envelopes off to one side. "Just wanted to see if there was anything that might interest you.

"Ah, how about this?" He picked up a thick paperback and fanned the pages. "It's one of my favorite books—Ernest Holmes's *The Science of Mind.*" He handed it to me. "Ever read it?"

"No."

"I just started reading it again for the umpteenth time."

"Looks like you've done more than that," I flipped through the well-worn pages. "It's all marked it up with highlights and notes."

"Yes, so many of these principles are worth underlining . . . they're what guided me while building Carter's Court. They helped me achieve my dreams—"

"And then you headed out to The Church Of Religious Science headquarters?"

"Yes—by the way, these days it's called United Centers for Spiritual Living—Marilyn and I just pulled up our roots and took off for the coast. I think some of the folks back home were very concerned. They thought I'd joined a cult or something."

"Really?"

"Yes, there was a rumor going around that I'd joined *Scientology*. Some even claimed I went to become their leader!"

"You mean like Tom Cruise and L. Ron Hubbard . . . Dianetics' Scientology?"

"Mm hm," he nodded. "In fact, I think that rumor is still circulating. I still hear people twenty-five years later thinking that Science of Mind is Scientology. It's totally different. Anyway, I didn't really mind what people thought of me. I knew I was headed in the right direction. I felt as if I was finally waking up to who I was meant to be. Instead of chasing money and big projects I was developing the spiritual leg of my tripod. That felt good."

"What were you learning?"

"Basically more of what I'd already been studying, but it was so inspiring to be around others who believed like myself. Back home there were so many naysayers, but these folks were real *can do* kind of people." Calvin pointed to a plaque on his desk. "See that? *Conceive, Believe, Achieve*. This is one of their sayings. There was also: *Picturize, Prayerize, Actualize*, and another one: *Be, Do, Have*."

"Very positive."

"They're all saying essentially the same thing. But when you examine them, you notice there's nothing in the future, nothing in the past—they are all in the present. It was Dr. Norman Vincent Peale who wrote *Picturize, Prayerize, Actualize*. I've had those words in my office for years. It's been a great reminder for me—a good way to break the habits of common, ordinary, everyday consciousness. And *Be, Do, Have* reminds you if you are *being* and *doing* you will *have*, because of the consciousness you're in."

"Ah," I smiled. "Now you're starting to sound like a motivational speaker."

"Well, that's what the folks at the Science of Mind thought too. They said, 'Mr. Lehew, you've done some remarkable things in creating wealth. You ought to speak to our groups . . . tell them how you've done this.'

"I said, 'I can't do that. I'm not a public speaker.'

But they kept encouraging me. They said, 'Use the principles we teach. See yourself speaking in front of people. You've got a great message to give these folks.'

I figured I might as well try it. And before long I was speaking on a regular basis."

"I bet you were a natural . . . "

"I'll admit, I really enjoyed it." Calvin faked a country twang, "They billed me as a *Suther'n redneck who b'came a million-airre* . . . and it really drew people in. At first I tried to get rid of my Southern accent until I realized it was one of the best things I had going for me.

"I remember once when I was speaking at a church in Northern California. The place was packed and I was up there in the pulpit speaking with great authority. ' . . . and Jesus says, *As a man thinketh in his heart, so is he* . . . '

"About that time, a little girl stood up in the audience and pointed her finger up at me. 'That was *not* Jesus, that was Paul!' The church fell silent. I was so embarrassed. I mean, *how do you recover from that?* I didn't know whether it was Paul or Jesus . . . it didn't matter to me. I just wanted to disappear.

But something took over me and I said to her, 'You are exactly right! And if I mess up like that again, please correct me.' I don't think I could've said anything better because I was suddenly aware that I'd gotten too big for my britches."

"Kind of humbling?"

"It was . . . " He chuckled. "And I learned my lesson. Funny thing, though—I discovered later that it wasn't really Jesus or even Paul who said that after all. It's in Proverbs 23:7."

I tried to imagine what those days were like for him. "I'm guessing it would be easy to get caught up in the glamorous lifestyle of California?"

"Yes," he said, nodding. "Not long after that, I costarred with Robert Stack and Della Reese in a film called *How to Change Your Life*. It won an Angel Award, which is sort of like an Emmy. And I'll admit, I really enjoyed being at the premiere.

"Around that time, I was also honored to do a speaking engagement with Buckminster Fuller."

"Sorry, but who?"

"Bucky Fuller, the famous architect and designer—inventor of the Geodesic Dome, which was based on the structure of an egg shell. He was one of the smartest men I've ever met. He was also known for having extrasensory perception and remote viewing abilities—he could see distant things without being there. I found it all fascinating. This man was so far ahead of his time and it was fun to be around him.

"Anyway, we'd been out in California for a while when we got a visit from some old friends, Ben and Betty, from Tennessee. Sometimes I wonder if they were sent as ambassadors to see what I was really up to . . . you know, with the Scientology rumor and all. Our first day together we were out having lunch when they began asking questions: 'Calvin, What are you really doing out here? What is all this Scien . . . Scien—'

"'Science Of Mind.' I said. 'Or Religious Science.'

"'Yes, Science of Mind. What exactly are you studying?'

"So I told them a little about it. Then I told them how they could do little exercises to stretch their own minds. One is learning how to 'manifest' parking spaces. I explained how to visualize the space in their mind and trust that it would be there when they arrived. Of course, after a while you graduate to bigger and better things. For instance, having someone you want to come into your life or getting a phone call from someone you want to talk to. You are literally bringing about what you think about.

"Well, Ben jumped right on this. 'I'd like to see Mary Tyler Moore while we're out here!'

"'Okay, Ben.' I said, 'Just put that thought in your mind and hold onto it and in a few days or so she'll show up.' Later, we paid our bill and headed out to the sidewalk. Almost immediately, we noticed a sporty Mercedes-Benz coming down the street. I thought, *Oh, my Gosh! It's Mary Tyler Moore! And she's coming this way!* Then she turned in the parking lot next to us. We watched, amazed, as she got out and went into a lingerie shop. Ben followed her right in!

"Betty couldn't believe it. She said, 'Okay, I want to see Robert Wagner.'

"'Alright then, Betty. Just hold that thought and picture Robert Wagner in your mind.'

"Later that night, we were out having dinner and Betty excused herself to go to the ladies room. On her way back to the table she passed a private dining room, and who do you suppose was in there?"

"I'm gonna guess—Robert Wagner?"

"Yep."

"That's unbelievable!"

"I know, but it's true. Betty was just beside herself."

I was still nodding in wonder when Calvin spun his chair around and, reaching into his bookshelf, pulled out an old cassette tape.

He laid it on the desk in front of me. "Here's a recording of one of my seminars at a retreat center called Asilomar in Northern California. I recorded it around that time and I think there's something on it where I'm talking more about *creative visualization*."

"Great! I'll listen to it on the way home." I glanced at my watch. Eleven o'clock. I picked up my purse, together with *The Science of Mind* book, which I also promised to read.

He gave me a hug. "Say, I didn't ask when you arrived but . . . how are you feeling these days?"

"Oh, pretty good. Thanks. I've been feeling very positive about my health." I held up Calvin's cassette, then slid it into my briefcase. "I'm going to start *visualizing* my healing."

"Good, good!" He put his hands in his pockets, watching me leave.

I was almost out the door when I stopped and turned back toward Calvin. "You still know how to inspire someone."

He smiled. "Isn't that what we're here for?"

———&&&———

may 11, 2009

*I*T'S A BEAUTIFUL DAY, *though a bit on the cool side, and the girls and I are attending an event at an area park. We sit in the sunshine on a homemade blanket sharing a picnic. It feels good to be outside again after the long winter. Taking turns lying in each other's laps, we play like puppies, teasing one another, untying shoes laces, and making silly jokes about ourselves. I like hanging out with my children and pray it will always be this way.*

"Hey, girls." I stand up. "I'm gonna go find a restroom. Be back in a minute." Heading out across the wide lawn, I pull my jacket to me to block the wind. I find the nearest bathroom, but it's closed for repairs. It's a big park so I keep walking. Finally, after about ten minutes, I see a porta-potty. Thank God.

Inside, the afternoon sun feels good coming through the blue plastic and suddenly I'm overwhelmed with a feeling of thankfulness. I'm reminded of Calvin who often talks about having an attitude of gratitude, no matter where you are.

I close my eyes. Thank You, God, for this day . . . for my family . . .

and for all the wonderful friends who've supported us during the challenges of the last year. And thank You for healing my body . . . *I no sooner think this, when a message comes to me, almost like a download:*

Pray not for the healing of your body but rather for the healing of your soul. For the body is temporary. But the soul is eternal. And with the healing of the soul the body will follow.

Stunned, I click open the door and step out into the bright afternoon light. Could it really be that simple? *Walking back to the girls, I replay this new message over and over, surprised this has never occurred to me before. Of course, the healing of my soul would be the ultimate healing—and one worth praying for. It reminds me of Matthew 16:26, which says:* What good will it be for a man if he gains the whole world, yet forfeits his soul?

I begin praying for a new kind of healing. Although I will continue with the alternative treatments, I feel less passionate in my attitude and diligence to these protocols. There is a tendency I've discovered—when we are ill—to obsess about the body at the very time when we need most to concentrate on our spiritual health. Could this be what Calvin means by the imbalance of the physical, mental and spiritual legs of our tripod? I still believe that taking care of my body is of great importance. But I'm also getting the message that if there is underlying illness of the soul—what Calvin might call "bad vibrations"—it can reverberate throughout the body, on a subconscious level, overriding even the most careful physical nurturing.

So, it's not just our thoughts that create our reality, but also our vibrations—our feelings. For instance, even though I might consciously desire a miraculous healing in my body, if I have deeply held feelings—like a strong fear that I will become sicker—I could sabotage my desire to be well. Still, how do I know what to do about my unconscious feelings if I'm not consciously aware of them?

Maybe this is what I am here to learn; how to consciously find a way to release all my old feelings or energy patterns—those fears about my health and money, and the negative feelings like guilt, anger, abandonment, grief, sorrow, hurt, and sadness. Maybe then I'll truly discover, what is good for the soul is good for the body.

Either that, or I'll admit that I'm just a crazy, middle-aged woman who has unusual spiritual experiences in the porta-potty. Who knows? At any rate, I suddenly feel more hopeful. As I approach the picnic blanket, I see a couple of young girls waiting for me. Their smiling faces remind me of something else that's good for the soul— giving love . . . and letting it come in.

chapter 28

conscious
dreaming

*Our lives and behaviors are more affected by the beliefs
we hold unconsciously than by the beliefs we hold consciously.*

—FROM CALVIN'S *MANIFESTING DREAMS*

I pulled out of The Factory's parking lot, turned left onto Liberty Pike
and pushed Calvin's cassette into my car stereo—one of the only
machines in our family that would still play the old format.

"*The metaphor of myself as a tripod is holding a camera—symbolic of
me, and the way I see life . . .* " Calvin began. "*and, if I want to see more
of the possibilities around me, this tripod, with the physical, mental, and
spiritual legs, needs to stay in balance.*"

That part was familiar, so I hit fast-forward.

" *. . . the Bible says, 'Be ye transformed by the renewing of your
mind.' How do we transform our minds? We reprogram our thinking by
using affirmations and visualizations. I mentioned that you need to set a
goal . . . That's the first thing you need to do. Next you've got to write it
down. This is important because it's visual. I set dates on my written goals,
and take them out once in a while to review them, to read, and to keep
updating the goals. One of the tools I use for visualization is a Treasure
Map . . . See, here's a picture of a fellow who's real slender. I used to weigh*

over 200 lbs., and I used that visualization to get my weight down to 145. I chose this photo of a guy in jockey shorts . . . and you can see they don't pick fat boys to pose for those shots . . . "

I heard the tinny echo of an audience laughing in the background.

" . . . I put this picture on the mirror, where I could see it regularly, so I could visualize my future self. Another trick is to use vivid colors and memorable graphics. I'm doing a lot of research in that area and I think we are just tapping into these techniques. Everything we will be tomorrow is based on what we visualize today. I read in a Psychology Today magazine that you should use pictures that make you feel something . . . that make you feel good. Just rip it out of the magazine . . . and by the way, make sure it's your own magazine."

More laughter.

"A few years ago, I found this photo of a beautiful sunset in an airline magazine . . . it made me feel so good. I just realized the other day that it's just like the sunsets I see from my condominium at Redondo Beach. And this is a picture of an airplane . . . I have a goal of having an airplane of my own one of these days. Now I'm probably contradicting myself when I say 'one of these days,' instead of seeing myself in it today, but it isn't priority-one . . . I have more important things to do before I get that airplane."

I smiled because I knew I was hearing what amounted to an old prophecy of what eventually came true for Calvin, after he attended to higher priorities.

"I haven't set the date for when I'll get it, but it's in there . . . Here's a picture of a man with a suede coat. It's been in here for at least a year. The reason I put that one in there, at least on a conscious level, was to try to look like that handsome guy because he's so slim and all . . . It's usually hidden behind other pictures but I came across it again the other day . . . and I wanted you to see what he's wearing . . . Look. I bought this coat last month, and I'm wearing it tonight. It's exactly like the one in the picture. It wasn't even conscious, because it wasn't about the coat."

There was another wave of laugher.

"The point I want to make here is that whenever I put a picture in here, I know I'm going to get it. This is important . . . Try to link the feeling when you set the goal . . . I wanted a Jaguar . . . and it's parked behind the building here right now."

The audience couldn't stop laughing now.

"But I got the picture of the Jaguar a year before I bought it. And I went into the showroom and I sat behind the wheel. I smelled the new car smell . . . a jaguar smells great when its new . . . I thought of finding a way to put that smell into aerosol cans."

Someone from the audience spoke up, *"They already have it . . . "*

Calvin shot back, *"They do? Well, they beat me to it . . . Anyway, try to get the feeling. Get all five senses involved when you are visualizing. Now I'm not just talking about physical things, I mean a great relationship, a home, a family . . . you've got to really see it in your mind, and feel it in your senses."*

Visualizing . . . I didn't do it on purpose nearly enough but there had been times in my life when I'd used it successfully. I visualized our children. I'd help visualize our home and what it would feel like, and how it would look. And though I'd never really put it together before, I realized I had even visualized my husband, Peter. In fifth grade I began drawing pictures of a handsome man with a beard. I drew him on everything, my notebook and test papers, even my hand. "This is what my husband will look like," I said, having no idea of the power of my words. I got what I wished for—and more.

"Another thing that's so important is self-image." Calvin continued. *"I could do a whole seminar on this one subject. Back when I was a bank director sitting behind a big desk I saw on a daily basis how critical this is. When someone comes in to ask for a loan it's so important to have a good self-image. What you think of yourself is exactly the way other people see you. And they will give you exactly what you think of yourself.*

"Picturization . . . is a real shortcut to getting anything you want. As

a man thinketh in his heart . . . *what he pictures in his mind, and feels in his heart, is what will come about.*

"The subconscious cannot reason . . . it will believe anything you put in it . . . So make that subconscious your servant, not your master . . . If you put in negativity, it will give back negativity. I learned that from experience, and believe me, it is true."

"Inventors do this all the time. Thomas Edison and Henry Ford KNEW their problems could be solved—even when other engineers told them it couldn't be done. And they succeeded.

"Many of the daily choices a person makes are based on inner images that he is unaware of. When an image, which a person holds in his or her mind, manifests in the outer world, then that person is a creator. And visualizing is a mechanism of his creation. This visualization becomes reality, and reality—as a person generally thinks of it—is a reflection of his internal images. Science and metaphysics are beginning to agree that each person has the power to create and change the world through visualization . . . the inner and outer become one. 'Imagination is more important than intelligence . . .' Einstein said that."

Calvin's cassette tape ended at about the same time I turned into my driveway. I had to admit; I was more than just a little inspired by the whole "visualization" idea. Not the first time I'd heard about it, but a timely reminder for me. And to hear it from the younger version of Calvin LeHew—before he even hit his stride in helping renovate my hometown of Franklin, Tennessee—was especially meaningful.

chapter 29

hold that
thought

We are born to create, and we can't help it. Why is that?
Because God, the great Creator, is in us.

—ERNEST HOLMES

I drove down the driveway of "Dream Acres," the name Peter and I gave the home we built ten years ago. Walking from the carport through the ivy trellis that links to the farmhouse, I entered our Amish country kitchen. I was reminded once again of the intense visualization it took for us to design and build the place from our own sketches and blueprints. We were living in the manifestation of our own creative visualization experiment. I realized that everyone does this on some level.

Settling into the floral-patterned glider Peter bought the day Grace was born, I pulled out the copy of *The Science of Mind* book that Calvin gave me. There were lots of markings and notes throughout the pages and, on the inside cover, his code for finding these notes—crosses, asterisks, and double-triangle stars. The one shaped like the Star of David with a dot in the middle meant a page was a spiritual bulls-eye and needed to be reviewed carefully. So, I was specifically guided to the following pages, with the notation of *Visualization*. ✡ ✝

✡ THOUGHTS BECOME THINGS; the Universal mind contains the essence of everything that ever was, is, or shall be . . . This is a new creation produced by the same Creative Force or Energy that produced all things.

✝ When we [pray], be specific. "Whatsoever things we desire" when we pray we should "believe we have them." . . . This is the whole secret, a complete mental acceptance and embodiment of our desires.

. . . If one were to make a complete mental picture of himself as he would like to be . . . he would demonstrate that the control of affairs is from within . . . and not from without . . . whatever exists as a mental picture in Mind must tend to, and finally does, take form if the picture is really believed in and embodied.[iv]

I paused to reflect on the deeper meaning of what I was reading. In other words . . . dreams come true! But, if that was really so, then it would follow that our negative thoughts would also take form. Still, I couldn't let go of the idea that there are some random things that happen from outside of our own thoughts—natural disasters, epidemics, careless drivers, wars, and random acts of violence. We can't control everything, that's for sure. But we do have power over our inner thoughts and how we respond to our circumstances.

We should be careful to distinguish daydreaming and wishing from dynamic and creative prayer . . . We do not expect something is going to happen; we BELIEVE IT ALREADY HAPPENED.

✡ ✝ Remember, when you use your subjective mind you use the Creative Power of the Universe . . . we should remind ourselves that it is not I but the Spirit of the Father in me who does the work.[v]

I tried randomly flipping through *The Science of Mind*, but found it pretty dense. Without some guidance, it was hard to unpack many of the concepts, deeply understood truths about how God uses our minds as vessels for His Mind—our spirit for His Spirit. I also imagined what a theological minefield this could be when trying to discuss it with some people. My heart was full of compassion for Calvin. I admired the courage it took, talking about these things in our religiously fundamental Southern town.

Later in the afternoon, I called to tell him what I thought about the seminar tape. But before I could say anything, he told me he'd gone out flying today.

"Were you up in your 'manifested' airplane?" I laughed.

"Yes, ma'am! It was a beautiful day."

"Well, I just wanted to tell you I listened to your tape on the way home and I love the idea about getting your senses involved . . . really visualizing and feeling whatever it is you want."

"Yes, and I think that's really one of the things Jesus tries to get across . . . He says, 'Have faith in God . . . I tell you the truth, if anyone says to this mountain, "Go, throw yourself into the sea," and does not doubt in his heart but believes that what he says will happen, it will be done for him . . .' Notice he says 'in his heart' . . . In other words you have to feel it and not just believe it in your head. And remember what the rest of that verse says?"

"Doesn't it say, ' . . . whatever you ask for in prayer, *believe* that you have *received* it, and it will be yours . . . ?' "

"Exactly . . . and that's the kind of teaching I got when I was out in California. It was really good for me to have all that stuff saturate my mind, because of what came later. I didn't know it then, but I was going to visualize some really amazing things into reality . . . and not just airplanes."

"Right," I figured he was talking about the renovation of Franklin. "How long did you stay out in California?"

"Oh . . . two years. It was a good time for us. Positive. But after a while it did start to lose its charm. As wonderful as everything was, an old feeling began to haunt me: *Is this all there is?* I guess I missed the creative process that happens when you're risking everything to start a new business. And maybe I was even drawing that situation to myself, because one day I got a call from a friend back in Franklin that changed everything again.

"I remember sitting in the Jacuzzi—like I did most evenings—drinking a glass of red wine, listening to my favorite Neil Diamond record, and enjoying a gorgeous sunset over the Pacific Ocean."

"Sounds perfect."

"It was . . . But just then I heard Marilyn calling from the house. 'Calvin, there's an old friend on the phone for you. It's Johnny Noel.' I didn't know it then but I was about to start a whole new chapter of my life . . .

Johnny said, 'I just thought I'd call and give you a heads up. Remember what you wanted to do with Franklin several years ago? The pretty sidewalks, cafés, and shops? Well, we can do it now. There are over twenty buildings for sale!'"

home again

Dreams do come true. This happens because dreaming involves visualization or inward imaging. The body, our physical house, is the servant of the mind.

—From Calvin's *Manifesting Dreams*

Calvin and I had been talking on the phone for the last twenty minutes. He was on a roll so I leaned back and made myself comfortable in an easy chair. I wondered what went through Calvin's mind when his old dream about Franklin suddenly came back to life.

"I was absolutely ready to go for it. Marilyn was too. So we headed back to Tennessee and bought seven buildings in downtown Franklin for $350,000."

"That's a lot of real estate for the money."

"Yes, and Johnny and another friend of ours, Ed Stahlman, also bought about that many. The three of us had a vision, but soon problems arose."

"Why?"

"We had what we thought was a great idea for the beautification of the downtown area . . . pretty sidewalks, trees, and streetlamps. It was called Streetscape, but it was difficult getting the new storeowners to agree to our plans. We needed 80 percent cooperation with all the owners to make Streetscape work."

"So, how'd you do it?"

"Word pictures. Being able to visualize something is powerful. So we convinced them by painting pictures in their minds of what we were planning to do. 'Imagine your family strolling past colorful flower planters; imagine shoppers casually strolling by, enticed by the aroma of fresh coffee wafting by vintage lamp-posts . . .' I'd already proven with Carter's Court that tourism could work—having beautiful sidewalks and cafés just seems to draw people in. It took a while, but they finally got on board.

"The next difficulty was bringing in restaurants. So once again, Marilyn and I jumped in and opened our own. And I'll say right now, she was the brain behind getting it up and running. But we needed a name for it.

"I was still doing speaking engagements out in California, and I remember walking down the streets of San Francisco one day, wondering what we should call our restaurant. All of the sudden, I was struck by how we have unlimited choices in life. Choices . . . "

"Choices Restaurant!" I suddenly made the connection. "We used to eat there all the time. In fact, I went into labor with our first child while we ate there one Sunday. Great food . . . and a good name, too."

"Marilyn liked it. The public might not have been aware of why we chose to call it that, but I liked giving the name a positive spin. We also opened a place above Choices to listen to music and have a drink. I named it Bennett's Corner because it was originally Bennett's Hardware store. I try to honor the history of places I restore.

"It wasn't an easy undertaking, but over time Choices became a big success. The restaurant business is still one of the worst businesses to be in, so many things can go wrong. But we kept the faith and it turned out to be a great experience.

"It was about that time, people around town began asking advice.

They wanted to know my secrets for success. So, I began giving seminars like I did back in California. In fact, I did a seminar called *Winning Choices*, playing off the popularity of our restaurant . . . "

Before I could say anything else, Calvin got another call. A quick good-bye and I hung up the phone, making a mental note to ask him more about that seminar later. It might come in useful.

june 27, 2009

I'M MAKING AN UNEASY CHOICE NOW; *I'm choosing to ig-nore the occasional pains in my rectum. And the bleeding. Maybe I'm being stubborn, but I cling to the belief that my body will heal itself. I begin each day by visualizing a long healthy life. Then I live as if there were no tomorrow.*

A gift has been offered to me—a chance to go to St. Augustine, Florida, for a couple of weeks. I'm taking it. This will be a chance for me to relax, do some writing, and spend some time with my new friend, Marilyn Edwards, who does healing work. I'm hoping she can help me get through any physical or emotional blocks that might be hindering my healing. She has a way of getting right to the heart of the matter.

"Do you love yourself, Stowe?" Marilyn asks. "I mean, really love yourself?"

"Yes," I answer too quickly. She studies me. Over the last few months, I've learned that Marilyn is one of those special people who has not only the gift of healing—what some call laying on of hands—but she also has the ability to see

beyond the surface—perhaps what's called the gift of knowledge. In other words, she intuitively knows what people are thinking. She is a wonderful listener too—good at reflecting thoughts back.

When I look in her eyes she smiles, and I have the feeling she is on to me. "You know," she says, "right now you look just like your daughter, Grace."

"Thanks . . . that's quite a compliment."

"Yes, she's a special little girl." Again, Marilyn studies me. She leans in closer. "You've told me about your past . . . how your mother died when you were young, how your father put you and your brother into foster care. And I know you were abused . . . emotionally and sexually . . . I can only imagine that throughout all that you must've felt abandoned . . . unloved."

"Yes," my voice is barely a whisper.

" . . . And, perhaps, as a child you thought that if the world didn't love you, if your family didn't love you . . . maybe you didn't deserve to be loved . . . "

My jaw tightens and I lower my eyes. The room suddenly feels hot.

"Am I right?"

I nod slowly.

"Okay, Stowe. I want you to do something for me. Close your eyes now . . . and imagine a few of the bad things that happened to you as a child . . . Can you do that?"

"Yes."

"Alright. Now I want you to imagine those things happening to Grace."

"Oh!" I cry out suddenly. "No . . . " Tears sting my eyes. This is an unbearable thought.

Marilyn reaches out to me, placing her hand on mine. "Okay . . . now I want you to see yourself as you see Grace . . . to picture the beautiful child that you are . . . love her like you love Grace."

I inhale deeply. In one incredible moment, Marilyn has made me see myself in a whole new light. It's as if I am peeking in through a window and seeing a lonely, little girl all by herself in the world. And for the first time in my life, I have sympathy for this child, the girl I used to be. I can see now that I wasn't a bad girl. I was just a girl that bad things happened to.

This change of heart feels like a miracle and, while it's not an overnight transformation, it does crack open the door to seeing myself from a different perspective. I approach the place where I can honestly appreciate who I am.

I've heard about people who are asked to look into a mirror and say, "I love you." For many, this is an almost impossible task. They often see only what they consider to be wrong with themselves. "My nose is crooked." "I hate these wrinkles." Or "I look old." Subconsciously, they may even see guilt, defeat, or judgment. I begin to wonder, how can we 'love one another as we love ourselves' when we're so busy criticizing or condemning ourselves?

I try looking in the mirror and, I admit, it does feel a bit awkward. But it's through the act of gazing into my own eyes and saying, "I love you," that I begin to get beyond the so-called flaws and blemishes and see a beautiful child of God. We've heard it said, "God don't make no junk." I believe that. I also believe that being aware of the child of God inside me helps me recognize all the other children of God I share this world with.

I reflect back on my recent struggles and I see that, if nothing else, these experiences are a second chance for me to learn to love myself. I feel grateful for this opportunity. My dear aunt, Jane Emery, recently told me, "I am realistic about human life but I believe that on the whole we get a lot more second chances than we realize; the friend you lost track of in adolescence returns to you on Facebook thirty-five years later; the passport you've been searching for shows up when you reach your hand into your old raincoat; you regain faith that has departed from you and sometimes . . . sometimes you even get a second chance at life." I agree with her. Our lives are filled with second chances.

Aunt Jane also told me another story about her husband, Clark, who died recently at the age of 100. The last few months were difficult for him— his ailing body, along with his memory, were giving out on him—but he still loved to read. Jane asked him one night, "How do you find pleasure in reading when you can't even remember what you've read?"

He gazed up at her and, with a wizened smile that was Clark's alone, said. "I enjoy the page I'm on."

We all want a little more time. But all we have is now. I believe when I acknowledge this, it's like receiving an unexpected gift—an opportunity to be in the moment. To sing and dance. To laugh. And to love, not only those around me, but myself as well. It's taking a deep breath, discovering the treasures of another day and delighting in knowing I am a much-loved child of God. And it's a second chance, as Clark said, to "enjoy the page I'm on."

Second Chance

Sitting in the backseat of my car
Strumming on my old guitar
Singing songs with my wooden friend
And thinkin' back a year ago it was almost the end

I still feel the echoes of the day I got the news
When it dawned I had everything to lose
By prayers of strangers and love of family
Everyday I walk this world is all a gift to me ('cause)

I got a second chance
To laugh and love
To sing and dance
And oh, I know it's a sweet and precious gift
A second chance to live

Some stay awhile some say good-bye
Who knows when who knows why
But we all have a chance to try
Learning how to love

When it's my time when all my work is done
He'll call my name and I'll be gone
And I'll finally see my Father's face
And stand before the love of His amazing grace

And I'll have a second chance
To laugh and love
To sing and dance
And oh, I know it's a sweet and precious gift
A second chance to live

partners
for life

*A wedding anniversary is the celebration of love,
trust, partnership, tolerance and tenacity.
The order varies for any given year.*

—PAUL SWEENEY

Often, Peter and I would be deep in conversation with Calvin when his wife's name would come up. Then, as if on cue, he would hold up his hand, "Listen, there's Marilyn now . . . down the hall." It amused me whenever he did that. After four and a half decades together, Calvin is very attuned to the sound of her voice.

"Hey," He pulled open his desk drawer, "Did I ever show you these?" Calvin held out several slips of paper.

"No," I leaned in toward his desk. "What are they?"

"Million dollar bank notes . . . reminders of some of the difficult times we've been through." He handed me the different colored pieces of paper. "Look at the interest rates . . . fourteen percent . . . fifteen percent . . . seventeen percent."

"They make our mortgage seem like chicken feed."

He took a deep breath. "Those were some tough times . . . and you notice whose name is there at the bottom . . . beside mine?"

My eyes fell to the signature. "Marilyn."

"Yes, she stood beside me during some of the most stressful periods of our lives, not only putting her faith in me on the line, but also her good name."

"That says a lot about her . . . " I handed back the bank notes. "And about your marriage."

"It does . . . and I want to say this; I don't give Marilyn near enough credit. But I owe her so much. I might be the front man, seeing the big picture, but she's the details person. She's the one in the background really making things happen. I couldn't have done any of this without her. She is to me like that old song, 'the wind beneath my wings.' "

They met back in 1962 on the famous boardwalk of Atlantic City, New Jersey. Calvin was attending a fraternity convention. Marilyn was on summer break from college—and for Calvin, it was love at first sight. He and a couple of buddies were cruising outside the clubs when he spotted Marilyn with two of her friends walking toward them. She was tall, dark-haired, and wearing a shirt with a West Point emblem—a school Calvin had dreamed about attending. As they passed one another, Calvin stood tall, and gave her a salute. She ignored him.

Calvin was undeterred. "Guys," he announced, "before this night is over I will be dancing with her!"

His friends laughed. But a few hours later, and a little further down the boardwalk, Calvin made good on his promise—he and Marilyn were dancing.

"And we've been dancing ever since." He grinned. "But, like any marriage, we've had our share of hard times. We're opposites in a lot of ways and maybe that makes for a good marriage, but it can also create a lot of tension. The main thing, though, is that our values are alike. We believe in our marriage and that is what's gotten us through the tough times."

"What do you love most about her?"

"I love her honesty . . . that she doesn't hide . . . "

"You know where you stand?"

"Yes." Calvin nodded. "I always know where I stand . . . though that's not always a good thing." He winked. "She's sincere, honest, and very much into giving to others."

I remembered the first time Marilyn and Calvin came to our home. She brought a basketful of exciting gifts to the children—several different crafts and homemade cookies.

"Her nature is to share," he continued. "She's a people person, she likes to be involved and work with others . . . even more than I do. She's a faithful, hard-working woman, very smart. And she's supported me in so many ways."

From the day Calvin and I met, our conversations had been sprinkled with the name *Marilyn*. He was quick to point out that every one of the major projects he'd done—Carter's Court, the renovation of downtown Franklin, and The Factory—had all needed restaurants. Risky ventures. And it was always Marilyn who was willing to do them. She was the one who got in the kitchen and worked, putting her heart and soul into them, making them successful.

"She also has a keen eye for décor," Calvin said. "She makes everything more beautiful, like the gardening and decorations around The Factory. Appearances are important to her." Calvin lowered his eyes, pointing to his flight suit. "I think I disappoint her a good deal with the way I dress."

Just then there was a light knock on the door. It was Marilyn. Calvin lifted his head. "Ah, there she is . . . " He put his hand to the side of his mouth and in a loud whisper, said, "Don't tell her we were talking about her."

I turned to greet Marilyn, whose arms were loaded with several baskets. She is tall with a bright smile, beautiful gray hair and a Pennsylvania accent; an energetic woman with an all-business kind of attitude.

She turned to face Calvin. "Sorry to interrupt . . . I just wanted to let you know your lunch is ready whenever you are."

"Okay, thanks." He motioned in the direction of her arms. "What's in the baskets?"

"Oh, just some Fourth of July decorations for Building 11 . . . " She turned to greet Peter and me.

"Hey, Marilyn," I said. "We were just talking about marriage and what makes a good one . . . you two have been married a while—"

"Forty-five years."

"Yes, and I was wondering, what do you think has kept you together all these years?"

Marilyn rested her baskets on the desk. "I know how long it took me to find Calvin and I'd have to say I made a pretty wise choice . . . " She paused, looking thoughtful. "But what keeps us together?"

Calvin jumped in. "I'd say respect. We respect each other and our opinions . . . that's how I see it."

"Well, the way I see it," Marilyn smiled, "I let Calvin get his way and I get to travel the world. We're both free to do what we like."

Calvin leaned back in his seat and folded his hands over his stomach. "I told Marilyn years ago, 'when we get married and we're above the Mason-Dixon Line, you're in charge of where, and how, and what we do. But when we go below the Mason-Dixon Line, Jesus and I are both in charge.' "

Marilyn shook a finger at him. "Yes, and you notice we've been down here most of the time . . . " Then she turned to me. "But when we're up there, believe me, he doesn't make any decisions." She glanced back at Calvin. "Maybe I need to take you up there more often!"

Calvin laughed softly and, sensing Marilyn was ready to go, told her he would be up soon for lunch. I watched her leave. Out in the hallway I heard her talking with the staff. This was the voice that Calvin knew so well, the one he'd listened to for all these many years.

"She's very youthful." I said. "Was she as pretty when you met her as she is now?"

Calvin nodded. "She was beautiful . . . still is."

"Forty-five years. That's a long time . . . "

"Yes, it is." Calvin took a breath. "We've been around the world with it, hard times and good times . . . "

"And you're still together."

"Mm hmm." He smiled. "Still together."

———— ∞∞∞ ∞ ————

the
natchez trace

*We plant a seed and a flower grows; we plant a thought,
an idea, and it manifests in our lives. Ideas are to
the subconscious what a seed is to the soil.*

—FROM CALVIN'S *MANIFESTING DREAMS*

We sat quietly for a moment. Calvin reached across his desk, slowly sifting through a stack of papers. He finally found what he was looking for and handed an envelope to Rod through the opening between their offices. I glanced around the room. A photo of Calvin standing behind a podium making a speech caught my eye. Clearing my throat, I asked, "Was that when Al Gore gave you the bodyguard pin?"

"Oh," he said, looking over his glasses. "Yes. That was the official opening of Natchez Trace."

"How'd you get involved with that?"

"Well . . . I've been fascinated with the Trace since I was a boy. I remember the old men sitting around on the porch of my father's general store telling stories about the Natchez Trail—that's what they used to call it. It was first a buffalo trail, then a footpath used by the Indians. Later it was a wagon road. In 1801 the Postal Service designated it as the official postal road to three different states. But after the steamboat was invented and cargo could be carried back and forth between the states, they stopped using it. As a kid, that part of the story always made me kind of sad.

"I remember there was one man in particular that used to visit my dad's general store. His name was Tommy Reese. One day I was just swinging on the pole—I was probably about nine years old—and I said, 'Mr. Tommy, I hear that some day they're going to make a parkway out of the Natchez Trail . . .'

"His eyes narrowed and he wagged his finger at me. 'Son, you'll never see that day. They'll never do it.' "

Calvin squeezed his eyes, bringing the memory closer. "There was something in the way he said it—"

"Like a challenge?"

"Yep . . . I imagine that was the day the seed was planted in me . . . Later on, I became president of the Natchez Trace Parkway Association and together, we helped complete the 444 miles of paved, scenic roadway from Natchez, Mississippi, to Nashville, Tennessee.

"The idea originally started about a hundred years ago by a group of ladies down in Natchez—the Daughters of the American Revolution—and they founded the movement to turn the trail into a parkway. I joined them back in 1988. I just wanted to do more for the community of my hometown, Leiper's Fork. But it wasn't easy . . . it took us until 2005 to get it done."

"A lot of hoops to jump through?"

He nodded. "First, each state had to get a special right-of-way. Then the three organizations in each state had to lobby the congressmen and senators to get appropriations. It was done in sections. Since the federal government owned it, they were in charge of the actual building and paving of the parkway. It took a lot of years to complete, but it's one of the things I've had a part in that I feel most proud of, because it benefits future generations."

"And that beautiful bridge on the Trace . . ." I tilted my head toward the picture. " . . . the one with the graceful arch . . . what about that?"

"That is one unique bridge," Calvin gazed at the picture. "It spans a great distance and is a tourist attraction in itself. The cost to build it was tremendous, so here's how I explained it to my congressman; I told him it was the cost of one fighter jet, and that it would be more beneficial in the future than any warplane."

Amazing. This was no small task to accomplish. It was another illustration of the visionary he is . . . seeing value in things of the past. Taking something old, and not only making it new, but bringing more value to the community by doing so. Like seeing diamonds in the rough.

I thought about his old cassette tape I'd been transcribing. What first seemed like just another motivational speech was now taking on a life of it's own. Hearing the real-life examples of how Calvin put these principles to work was like putting meat on the bones of all his success seminars.

As I pulled out of the parking lot that day, I slid his tape in the player and immediately joined Calvin's audience as he spoke about cause and effect.

"*Everything in this room,*" he began, "*and most everything you ever see, is an effect. And there's a cause behind every effect. Consciously or unconsciously.*"

He spoke with the passion of a preacher: "*Jesus says the symbol of the seed is the first cause: 'faith is like a mustard seed.' This is hard, sometimes, for people to grasp. A philosopher might say this object in my hands isn't 'reality,' although I perceive it as real. The real thing is the invisible, the idea . . . the word. It all begins here.*

"*Look around. These are all just things and have no power in themselves. Everything we see here in this room was first an idea in somebody's mind. The building where this meeting is held was just a thought, at first. The idea was the first creation. Things are effects—they have no power in themselves.*"

"*Everything in the Universe was originally created from an Intelligent Source we call God. And everything that humans create is created* from their own intelligence. Remember . . . we are created in God's image, as intelligent creators. And how does intelligence begin creating anything? Through the Word! 'In the Beginning was the Word . . . and the Word was God.' "

"Amen!" A voice from Calvin's long ago audience chimed in.

"And it goes on to say that 'through him, [the Word] all things were made; without him nothing was made that has been made.' All throughout the Bible, the Word is all about creating something new. The word you speak is a mold that creates form—it gives birth; it creates. That's called 'first cause,' or the creation behind what's created.

"The image in the mind, when expressed by the word, is the first cause. What you think about, you bring about. Be it negative or positive, 'By your words you are acquitted and by your words you are condemned.' The Word is powerful.

"Any real estate or salesperson knows they have to see the invisible. All creation starts from the invisible and goes to the visible. For instance, our Choices Restaurant . . . this was first an idea, which was spoken aloud. Then it went onto paper, a blueprint—a plan. Then it became bricks and mortar, concrete, light fixtures, and so on. The idea became effect. This is how we create anything. This is the secret of success."

"Think about what you want. Express it in words. Make a plan, and then go for it. Automatically, your subconscious will take over from there and you won't have to worry too much about creating the effects. When you have your plan, you can just believe and things will start miraculously happening. Get clear on it, and then get out of the way. This is where miracles start taking place."

He finally paused and I could almost see him looking out into the faces of his audience. He had, no doubt, preached this message to many. But alone in my car that day, I felt that message was only for me. Did I have the faith to do what I needed to do?

"'According to your faith,'" he had said earlier, slowly and with great sincerity, "'is it done unto you.' This is my message today. Belief and faith are invisible. They are not an effect, but the cause behind all that happens."

I definitely got the message from Calvin that faith is the invisible cause behind the eventual effect. Like the Bible says, "Now faith is the substance of things hoped for, the evidence of things not seen." But I also saw from his life example that faith is about doing—how you act, not just how you believe. I could see, time and again, that he put forward his intentions, then acted upon them, believing in what he was doing. And if the magnificent Natchez Trace Bridge symbolized anything, it was how an idea or thought could gracefully and successfully span the difficult challenges of taking a plan from inception to completion.

I'd like to share a footnote to this chapter about the Natchez Trace, and the impact of Calvin's teachings. Knowing her interest in Tennessee history, Calvin gifted our fourteen-year-old daughter, Christina, with a book—a photo essay on the Natchez Trace. After reading it, our family took a weekend trip down the beautiful parkway and stayed overnight at a cabin beside a pond stocked with catfish.

The next morning Peter and Christina went fishing, hoping to catch something for lunch—but no success. Later, they tried once more. But again, scarcely a nibble, although they'd seen a swarm of large catfish when the cabin's owner had thrown out a handful of—what else—cat food. "Keep trying," Peter told Christina. "I'll go pack up the car for the trip home."

When we returned fifteen minutes later, she'd finally caught a fish and was very excited. "Can I try again, so we can have enough for dinner? Please?"

We stood by, anxiously awaiting a bite as Peter preserved the moment with his video camera. Suddenly, the bobber disappeared. Christina reeled in a big catfish—only to watch it get away at the shoreline. She flashed a frown, then begged for one more chance.

Once again, Peter filmed the scene, which repeated exactly as the first, but this time Christina pulled the big fish onto the bank for keeps.

With the camera still rolling, she breathlessly exclaimed, "You don't even know the whole story! With the first fish, I said 'God, thanks for the fish that's about to get hooked.' When the bobber went under, I reeled it in. But just when it came to shore . . . it got away." Christina looked down at her fish and took a deep breath. "I realized I needed to be more specific. So I said, 'Thank You, God, for the fish that's going to get hooked, reeled to shore, and stay on shore!' "

I asked where she got the idea to be *specific*? She looked at me curiously, as if I should know. "I was listening," she reminded me, "when you transcribed Calvin's taped seminar. He said to *be specific when you pray* . . . so I gave it a try." The result was a great dinner.

But that's not all. The next day Christina took a walk by our creek bed in search of arrowheads. Several years had passed since she and Grace had found any there, but on this day, Christina remembered her 'gratitude' lesson from the day before.

You've probably already guessed the next scene. Christina ran in from the yard. "Guess what?" She held her hand behind her back. "I was down at the creek and I just finished saying, 'Lord, thank You for the arrowhead I'm about to find.' I turned around and looked down—"

"Alright . . . " Peter held his hand out. "Let me see it." Christina gave him a perfectly-formed, beautiful old arrowhead.

It shows how the power of our words, our prayers, and our thanksgiving have a life of their own. And whether or not we realize it, others may be listening—and learning.

Oh, did I mention that the Natchez Trace was originally an old Indian trail? It was used by hunters and traders—perhaps traveled by the same creator of Christina's ancient memento—a reminder to always be expectantly grateful.

chapter 34

september 7, 2009

*O*UTSIDE, THE SUN IS SHINING *brightly and my children, drawn instinctively to it, are somewhere out in the fresh air. While inside, in the cool darkness of my room, I'm reading everything I can about the incredible healing abilities of the human body and the power of the mind to bring it about.*

But something is wrong. Day by day, I am losing my energy. At times, it is almost beyond my ability to imagine my body healing. I need someone to talk to . . . Moments later my prayer is answered—the phone rings. It's probably no coincidence that my friend, Marilyn Edwards, the one with a profound spiritual gift of healing, calls just when I need her most. She's intuitive like that.

"So what's going on with you, Stowe?"

"I don't know . . . " My voice is weak, trembling with emotion. "It seems like I'm doing everything possible to facilitate my healing in a natural way . . . but at the same time I'm losing my strength. One day I feel like I'm healing, the next it feels like I'm dying."

"Do you want to live?"

"What kind of question is that?" I am defensive. "Of course I do."

"Why? . . . Tell me why you want to live."

"Well . . . I want to be here to help raise my children—I don't want them to be motherless like I was. And I want to be here for Peter. I want to do things with him . . . you know, travel and things like that. And . . . uhm . . . I'd like to do something with my music . . . "

And then I have a strange sensation—as if I'm a fly on the wall, a temporary observer of my conversation. I listen intently to the words I speak . . . and, more importantly, to how I say them. What's wrong with me? Where is my passion? *That's when I come to an uneasy realization—something is desperately lacking in me—a strong commitment to the act of living.* Why is that? What's happened to me?

winning
choices

Certain thoughts are prayers. There are moments when,
whatever be the attitude of the body, the soul is on its knees.

—Victor Hugo

I wanted a miracle. Now. *Where was it?* The truth was becoming pain-fully clear. I was not getting better. In fact, I was in bed for most of every day. The only times I left the house anymore were Monday mornings to meet with Calvin. My daily two-mile walks, a twenty-year routine, were no more. No more aerobics. No more weight lifting. Now I struggled just to sit in a chair. Lying down wasn't much better. And to top it all off, I had—under much protest—begun taking pain medicine.

Not surprisingly, I was also dealing with depression. I had tried everything, short of surgery, to bring about my healing. Yet here I was, getting worse by the day. Prayer, special diets, vibrational medicine, a plethora of pills, healers, hypnosis, flower essences, chemo, radiation, and positive thinking. Where had all of this gotten me?

I was losing hope. Who was I to think I could co-author a book on positive thinking? I was losing sight of everything, slipping into an abyss of pain. Up until recently, writing this book had been inspirational to me. Now, it was a burden. What was I going to do?

I stared down at Calvin's cassette tape on the coffee table in my sun-room. *Winning Choices.* It seemed to be mocking me. But since it was easier for me to transcribe a seminar than to write something new, I pushed the old cassette into the player. I needed some words of encouragement.

"*I want to talk about conscious awareness,*" he began. "*The definition of awareness is, 'The degree of clarity to which we perceive both consciously and unconsciously all the things that affect our lives.'*

"*I used to ask myself, why aren't more people trying to get ahead and achieve more things? I think the answer is because they aren't consciously aware of the many things that affect their lives, and the many choices they have under their own control. They would rather stay in their familiar comfort zone.*

"*I've come to believe that it's okay for people to stay in their comfort zone . . . if they want to. Those people are either happy where they are, or they don't know or believe these principles about conscious choices.*

"*Here's something else that bothered me for a long time: Why didn't God build us with total conscious awareness to begin with? The answer is: We had to have total freedom to discover these things on our own, or we wouldn't be free. It couldn't have happened if we weren't free to fall down and be hurt. To be bored enough to learn new things. Or to take risks by faith and then succeed. What is faith without freedom to choose? The answer is in the Bible. And, by the way, the principles I live by are all in the Bible.*

"*Making choices is the key after becoming aware. Being aware of our choices. The choices you make—either consciously or unconsciously—are affecting your life. You are responsible for the choices you make. From the clothes you wear, to the dollars in your bank account, to your job, to where you live—these are all the result of choices you've made. You are either happy or sad because you choose to be.*

"*I chose the name Choices for our restaurant because of this, not because of the variety of foods . . . it was because of the importance of this concept. We have literally hundreds and thousands of choices every day, and most people don't even realize it.*

"Most of us are content to stay in our comfort zones . . . we get stuck there. Part of the reason for this has to do with fear. It's scary to get out of your comfort zone. You've probably heard of people who stay in abusive marriages because they're afraid to change their situation—even though they don't like it, it's familiar.

"I understand this. I get comfortable too. But when I become aware of it, I try to pioneer out so I can experience something new.

"So many folks are unconscious of the fact they are stuck in habits, customs, old beliefs . . . How much of what we do is based on these routines? I'm not saying traditions are bad . . . Rituals are great, if we don't forget the meaning behind them. Christmas is great, as long as we don't forget why we celebrate it. But the routine of worrying—that's a destructive habit. Think about people you've known—maybe even yourself—unaware that doubt and worry control your life. Most of the time we're not even aware that we're unaware! We're oblivious to the fact that we have choices. But as your awareness increases, you become conscious that you are choosing where you are going.

"As I increase my awareness I begin to see, 'Gosh, I did allow that to happen to me. I did create that problem.' And I realize I am responsible for my situation . . . responsible for my actions. Responsible for the opportunities I didn't take advantage of. Responsible for the things I did and said.

I stared at the tape player and shifted in my chair.

"There was a time at Carter's Court when I almost lost everything. I got into alcohol—Jack Daniels. I started drinking around 5 o'clock in the evening. And it was all because I had fear. I almost gave up. Over the years I survived several plane crashes; I nearly cut my leg off with a chain saw. And I don't think these were accidents. I believe, on some level, that when we start giving up, we self-destruct. That's what I was doing. In many ways we create our own sickness . . .

"But, thank God, we have choices. And with that knowledge we can create the life we want. As children, our parents and teachers—the adults in our lives—make most decisions for us. We don't have much to say about *what happens. When we grow up though, we become responsible for our own lives. Yet many of us still continue to let other people or circumstances make decisions for us, either consciously or unconsciously.*

"Hopefully, what you'll get out of this message today is to start consciously choosing your life the way you want it. No doubt, most of us are in a comfort zone, but it's a great day to begin consciously making choices."

I clicked off the tape. I needed that reminder—I'm in control of my own choices. I'd made so many about my health over the last year and a half. Some good. Some not so good. Some were made from a place of love. Some from a place of fear. I could see that the choices made from fear—fear of surgery, for instance—were the reason for the shape I was in now.

Maybe, on some level, I was—like Calvin suggested—"giving up." He talked about "self-destructing." That made sense. But that thing he said about "creating our own sicknesses" had me puzzled.

I could understand how a person might choose to abuse their body by drinking too much alcohol or overeating. That kind of lifestyle could eventually lead to sickness or even death. And a person engaging in risky activities is also upping the ante that they'll be injured or killed. And those high-stress jobs some people have? Yes, they could certainly cause a heart attack.

I've known financially strapped men who made comments about having a heart attack, saying their families would be better off with the money from their life insurance policy. Maybe they were, on some level, either consciously or unconsciously, bringing that fate on themselves.

But did I really *choose* to have cancer? That was a hard one for me to buy into. Perhaps it was the result of past choices . . . who can say? But one thing was becoming clear: It was entirely up to me to decide how I would choose to—or not to—treat the cancer growing in me.

december 9, 2009

"*WOULD YOU LIKE me to give you the number for hospice, Stowe?*" *The room falls silent. Dr. Serie, my oncologist, observes me with genuine concern. "They'd be able to help with your pain . . . "*

"Hospice?" Are we really having this conversation? I shift uneasily in my chair, trying to relieve the pressure on my rectum. What should I say? "Uhm, . . . I—"

"Look," she leans in closer, "I know when most people think of hospice, it's because the patient is very close to the end of life."

"Right . . . "

"But they're actually quite helpful with pain management—I think that's where you could benefit. In fact, I've known them to work with patients for as long as two years . . . " She pauses, respecting the delicacy of the subject. "So . . . would that be something you'd like me to arrange?"

Peter and I exchange glances. I can tell he's anxious. Still, somehow, he manages to conduct himself in a business-like manner. "Yes, Doctor," he reaches out to take a card from her. "We'd appreciate that."

How has it come to this? How have I have gone from ardently pursuing living to actually embracing dying? Overwhelmed with unending physical pain, I've become a fatalist. It's all surreal . . .

My days are a blur of hours spent in the bathroom and the rest of the day lying in bed, recovering from what happens in the bathroom. I get up to do something only to walk a few steps and lie down on the nearest sofa or bed. Gone are the days of sitting at the dinner table with my family. It's too painful. And even if I could it wouldn't matter—I have no appetite. I've lost almost twenty pounds in the last four months. Maybe it's because of the heavy pain meds. Maybe it's the cancer. All I know is I'm in pain—and despite how it hurts my family—I can't stop moaning. It feels like I'm out of control, like I'm headed downhill in a car with no brakes.

Had it really been just six months since I was regularly performing my music? Back then I was writing a song one week and singing it the next. I was connecting with the audiences and sure I'd finally found myself.

Last summer, I was strong enough to take a two-week vacation with our family, which, at the time, included Cate, our wonderful foreign exchange student from Germany. We had a ball traveling from place to place, visiting relatives and playing in the warm waves of the Gulf and the Atlantic Ocean.

But even then, there were ominous signs of what was coming. Like the day at Universal Studios when I almost passed out after a short walk. I protested, but Peter called a paramedic and I was sent back to my hotel room to recuperate.

And so it went. Increasing pain. More bleeding. I watched my energy slip away. I didn't want to admit to anyone, even myself, that the alternative treatments I was doing weren't working. I was desperate to believe I could be made well through any means other than chemo, radiation, or surgery.

Now, the end of the year has arrived and a strange new thought comes to me: Maybe, I'm not supposed to live a long life. Maybe . . . this is how I'm going to die . . . *a horribly sad thought—leaving my family alone—knowing how it will hurt them. At the same time, the thought feels somehow peaceful. So I begin, gently at first, talking about it.*

Peter and I discuss the children; how he might raise them as a single father. We even talk about him remarrying someday, though I have little success in picking out a new wife for him. We talk about the completion of this book since there is the possibility he may have to finish it for me. And, throughout all these conversations, we cry.

I am forced to choose now if this will be the beginning of the end. No doubt, it is the eleventh hour for making a difficult choice. For months I've been adamant about not wanting to do the very thing that might save my life—having colostomy surgery. And now, I can't help but wonder: Have I waited too long?

---

cancer and
taking inventory

There is much in the world to make us afraid.
There is much more in our faith to make us unafraid.

—FREDERICK W. CROPP

Christmas was in the air. I dug my hands into my winter coat and shuffled toward The Factory. Peter—my friend, husband, and more recently, my caretaker—walked alongside me, holding my arm and carrying my briefcase. Inside the atmosphere was festive—a sign that Marilyn LeHew had been here—and twinkling lights along with ornamental wreaths lined the hallways. We climbed the stairs slowly to the strains of *Jingle Bell Rock* and rounded the corner of Calvin's office.

"Merry Christmas!" Peter called.

"Ho, ho, ho." Calvin rose to greet us. He hugged me gently. "How are you feeling?"

I blinked hard, trying to hold back the tears. "Not so great," I mumbled. I usually tried to keep my words positive around Calvin but I couldn't do it anymore. He stood until I was seated, no doubt concerned but at a loss for what to say.

As I lowered myself slowly into the chair I thought about Calvin's cancer. We had discussed it before—his had been in the prostate—yet for some reason we'd never delved too deeply into the details. I'm not sure why. Maybe we were always too caught up in the present moment. But today I struggled with what to do about my own cancer. I needed some encouragement.

I exhaled softly. "I'd like to . . . if it's okay with you . . . talk about your cancer experience."

"Alright . . . " He put his fingers together and raised them to his lips. "What do you want to know?"

I wasn't sure whether I wanted to talk about his cancer or mine. The lines were blurred. So I just jumped in. "What was going on with you around the time you were diagnosed?"

Calvin cleared his throat. "Oh, it was the normal, competitive, business-as-usual way of life. I was in the old routine of construction and working at The Factory."

"Just busy making money?"

"Yes," he picked up a stack of bills lying on the desktop. "When you owe ten million dollars for a development like this, there is *some* stress." He laughed at the understatement. "I just didn't realize how *much* stress I was under."

"Did you have any symptoms?"

He shrugged. "I guess my first clues might have been those mental and physical legs of my tripod . . . I was starting to feel down. I didn't have much energy. Marilyn suggested I go to the doctor. That's when they found out I had cancer."

"How'd you feel? I mean, what did you think when they told you?"

"Well, it didn't feel like such a big deal at first. I decided to make the best of it and had the surgery to remove my prostate. But then I had another meeting with the doctor. There was more bad news." Calvin sighed. "By then I just wanted to get it over with."

I nodded, remembering that same feeling. "So, what happened?"

"The doctor told me he wasn't able to get all of the cancer . . . and that my PSA levels weren't coming down. He even thought it might have metastasized. They recommended either chemotherapy or radiation. I knew the effects of chemo so I chose to have thirty-eight radiation treatments instead.

"Afterwards, I went out to the farm to be alone. I realized everything was changing. I was at a critical point in my life—a crossroad. And I guess I'm kind of still going through that right now. It's like, *What's left in life?* And maybe the answer is to help teach other people what I've learned so far. I want to tell them, 'You might be diagnosed with cancer or something else . . . you could be told you have only so many days to live.' I want to remind them to live every day like it's their last . . . " Calvin stopped. He folded his hands on the desk and looked me in the eyes.

Suddenly it felt as if I were caught in the glare of a spotlight. I said nothing, afraid I'd cry.

Finally, he spoke. "What's going on with you, Stowe?"

My face was hot. Tears welled up in my eyes. And the words I'd held inside for so long tumbled out of me like water over a falls. "I don't know what to do anymore. I've tried every alternative treatment I can think of . . . I've tried keeping my thoughts positive. I'm always thanking God for healing me . . . in a miraculous way. That's the goal I made last summer—to be miraculously healed by December. Now it's almost Christmas and . . . "

"What?"

"I went to my oncologist the other day . . . She gave me the number for hospice . . . " I sniffed. "Nothing's working . . . I'm dying."

Calvin shifted his eyes upward, as if searching for the right words. Neither of us spoke for what seemed like an eternity. Finally, he broke the silence. "Stowe . . . " He said gently. "It's not for us to question how this is going to resolve . . . how your healing is going to come about. I've found it's best to leave the *how* to our higher power. In some ways this reminds me of when I was learning about fire walking. We were specifically instructed to *keep our heads up.* Looking down would only cause us to concentrate on the hot coals. When facing fear, focus your attention on God. Not on yourself. Our minds are so powerful. If we think only about what's wrong or could go wrong—like the hot coals burning beneath our feet—we'll get burned.

"Look up and remember that Jesus taught us we can be healed. But it's not for us to determine how it will happen. Turn this around and don't decide for yourself *how* it's going to be done but let God do this. Let the Spirit lead you."

I understood about being led by the Spirit. But I also knew how terrifying it was to face cancer. And since fear is a self-centered emotion, it's difficult to be fear-ful and Spirit-led at the same time. I wondered how Calvin handled this during his surgery and radiation treatments.

"I made a mental decision," he said, "to try and enjoy the moment—like I learned to do during my out-of-body experience, when I was crashing in the airplane and thinking, *This is what it's like to die*—I just tried to stay aware enough to enjoy the experience when possible. "When I faced the cancer, I had a choice; do I go into doom and gloom or do I face it and see something different?"

"How'd you do it?"

"I tried to find the humor in it. I was deep in the middle of adversity—'*Man, you've got cancer!*' I'll never forget going into the cancer clinic with Marilyn. There were Kleenex boxes everywhere . . . and support groups you could join. The first time we went, there was a lady reading from a book, telling us all the things I was going to face—what I should and should not do. It was all so serious and sad." Calvin slumped his shoulders and hung out his tongue. "Afterwards she said, 'Do you have any questions, Mr. LeHew?'

"I just looked at her and said, 'What's for lunch?' " Calvin laughed. "You should have seen her face. She said, '*What?*' I thought, *This is too heavy*. They didn't understand me. I was trying to have fun, like I always try to do under pressure. Again, 'with every adversity . . . ' "

I knew that Calvin and I received radiation at the same clinic so I wondered about his experience. "What was it like for you?"

"The first thing they did was put me up on this board . . . and I was *neck-id*. I mean, I was totally *nude*. And the doctor comes in with a nurse. Her name was Jill.

I nodded, remembering Jill and her male counterpart, Jack. Jack and Jill. Now that was funny.

"So, they hadn't given me any kind of anesthesia and the next thing I knew, they were in front of me putting this tube up my you-know-what. It was very painful—*oh, man!* But I'm a macho guy, so I couldn't show any strain or signs of pain. Jill's sweet gaze seemed to say, 'I'm so sorry.' But then she pushed that thing some more . . . " Calvin shuddered at the memory. "I was determined to make the best of a bad situation. I focused on her pretty eyes and how beautiful she was. I tried joking with her, but it just went over her head.

"The next day I was on the table again—*nude*—and it was just Jill and me. She took a magic marker and, going about my privates, made little drawings where they were going to be shooting those rays. So I said, 'Jill, while you're down there, would you mind putting down your telephone number?' Dead silence. No smiling, no laughing. Nothing. So I let it go. Then, the next day, she took a photograph of me down there, for future reference.

"After I put my clothes on I went around to the front desk, where Jill and a couple of other people were standing. I said, 'Folks,' " Calvin made a face like an angry customer. " 'I want to register a complaint.' " He mimicked their shocked reactions. "That really got their attention. So I said, 'Jill, here, sexually molested me. She drew pictures on my privates, and then she took pornographic photos of me . . . and I *don't* want to see anything showing up on YouTube!' "

I laughed out loud.

Calvin nodded. "Yeah, I finally got a laugh out of them too. They're not used to people seeing the positive or even the humorous part of cancer . . . So that would be my advice to you, Stowe. Change your perspective . . . and your attitude about the situation."

I shifted uncomfortably in my chair. "But I'm not sure how . . . I just don't want to have surgery. I don't have faith in that or any of the standard treatments . . . "

"Well, maybe you don't have to have surgery."

I dropped my head. "But if I don't, I think I'm going to die."

"You have a choice. You don't have to die. You can have surgery and come through it. I did. Just remember, it's not for you to determine how you're going to be healed . . . "

I sniffed, echoing softly, "It's not for me to determine how I'm going to be healed."

"No." He said. "In everything I do. . . and every project, I envision the end result. But I don't tell God how I'm going to arrive at the end result. That's for a higher power than you or me to determine."

I took a deep breath. What he said made sense. And although I wasn't consciously aware of it at that moment, I think something *clicked*. "Thank you, Calvin."

He closed his eyes and bowed his head. "You're welcome."

What Cancer Cannot Do

AUTHOR UNKNOWN

Cancer is so limited . . .
It cannot cripple love.
It cannot shatter hope.
It cannot corrode faith.
It cannot eat away peace.
It cannot destroy confidence.
It cannot kill friendship.
It cannot shut out memories.
It cannot silence courage.
It cannot reduce eternal life.
It cannot quench the Spirit.

may 5, 2010

*T*HIS IS THE FIRST PAGE *I've written since January. The last few months are a blur. Did the scenes that haunt my mind really happen? Or was it just a bad dream? I draw my hand to my abdomen, feeling the pouch attached to my body beneath my clothing. Yes, it all really happened.*

I'm still sorting through the emotions and physical changes that occurred over the last few months. And since writing usually helps me give voice to those feelings that are buried, today is a day of reflection. So here goes . . .

We had been deep into one of the snowiest Januarys we'd had in years. Outside my window, snowflakes swirled with light-hearted abandon, then gently settled on our back porch. From my makeshift sickbed in the sunroom, I watched the snowflakes fall, hypnotized by the winter wonderland. Usually, I would have been tempted to play, at least throw a snowball or two with my children. But not that day. On that day I felt only the cold bitterness of winter and the heavy burden of a decision that fell solely on my shoulders.

Calvin had talked a lot about choices. We make them every day. Some are almost inconsequential—Should I wear the blue shirt or the green?

Coffee or tea? *Those are the easy ones. But there are some choices that affect more than just our self. They impact those around us, now and in the future. Choosing is like throwing a pebble into a pond and watching the ripples spread outward, across the water. It's anyone's guess how far the consequences of these decisions will run.*

This was the kind of choice I faced. I was choosing between having major surgery to remove my rectum and the cancer, or holding onto my fear and distrust of allopathic medicine and dying a slow, painful death. I stood at the edge of the future, my decision in hand, poised to toss it into life's still pond, and let the ripples run—knowing the choice I made would affect more than a few lives.

On the surface it sounded pretty obvious—have the surgery. So what if I had to wear a bag the rest of my life? And even if the operation was no guarantee for a long life, there was at least the hope I could spend a few more years with my family. I wanted that. But inside me a war was raging. I had seen firsthand the broken promises of chemo, radiation, and surgery, the celebration parties—doctors exclaiming, "We got it all!" And then months later—"We're sorry, it's back again . . ."

It all boiled down to this; I didn't trust modern medicine. How could I be sure that I wouldn't just end up in worse shape? I couldn't. There was no way, with my limited earthly vision, that I could predict the outcome.

But if I'd learned anything from Calvin concerning goal setting, it had to do with me not trying to dictate how I would arrive at that desired goal. I should just keep moving toward the destination of my dream, staying open to winds of change. After all, we don't always get there as the crow flies. Sometimes our higher guidance takes us on a course we hadn't anticipated.

So the bigger question became: Can I trust God? Can I believe there is an ultimate and perfect plan for me and my family? With that line of thinking, I began praying. In a few days I had my answer and with it, the peace I needed to move forward. I remember the night I told Peter.

"I've made my decision," I whispered.

"What are you going to do?" I could tell he was bracing himself.

"I'm going to . . . " I swallowed hard, " . . . do the surgery."

"Oh . . . thank God." He broke into tears. His voice choked, "Thank God."

Saying those words out loud was incredibly difficult, but once I made up my mind, I resolved to do it with humor. "Ain't no drag . . . " I sang in a wobbly voice, "Mama's got a brand new bag!"

That was the beginning of my long road to recovery. Nervous about the operation, I braced myself for what lay ahead. The five-hour surgery sounded scary, but even more frightening was the future. Statistically, a colostomy operation gives a person a thirty-five to sixty-five percent chance of living five years. Not bad odds. Still, I worried. And then I remembered a quote by David Kessler in Alana Stewart's book, My Journey with Farrah. "Fear doesn't stop you from dying; it stops you from living."[vi] That spoke to me. So I decided that with whatever amount of time I had left I would live life to the best of my abilities.

The weeks leading up to the surgery were difficult. Cancer can be painful and for me it was a merciless invader—unrelenting in its quest to defeat me. My once-toned body had atrophied and my wrinkled skin hung loosely on my frame. By day, I writhed in my makeshift sickbed in the sunroom, equipped with a heated amethyst mat to soothe the pain. At night, Peter lay in our bed—all alone—crying as he listened to me moan myself to sleep in the other room. What little energy I had was fading. There were times when I wondered if I would even make it to my surgery date.

Reflecting back, I realize how important friends and family were to me during that time. Their prayers lifted me in unexplainable ways and their bedside visits brought me joy. Holding hands and laughing with a loved one really does cheer the soul. In mid-February, our German foreign exchange "daughter," Cate, whom we hosted the year before, returned to America along with her mother and sister. She realized it might be our last chance to see each other again. Seeing her bright, smiling face and feeling her family's love was wonderful, and their presence also gave Peter and the girls emotional support as we approached the big day.

February 17th dawned, cold and cloudy. I packed my bag to go to the hospital. My memories of that day are like a patchwork quilt: kissing the sweet faces of my family and waving good-bye; hugging my friend, Mary Jane, at the hospital; laughing at anything—a nervous laughter that comes when something momentous is about to happen; the nurse calling my name— "Shockey . . . Mrs. Shockey!"; lying on the gurney and watching Peter text someone because he'd lost his voice. The added strain of caring for me over the last few months had finally taken its toll on his body—he was exhausted. The final square of the quilt was Peter's kiss and whisper of, "I love you" as I drifted off into a drug-induced sleep.

My new life began when I came back to consciousness, around eight-thirty that night. The surgery was successful—they got it all. I no longer had excruciating pain in my rectum. Now I had excruciating pain in my abdomen. But this would pass. Good friends got me through the first difficult nights. I made it a goal to heal quickly and set records by doing laps around the nurse's station. The normal hospital stay for colostomy surgery is five to seven days. I was released on the morning of the third.

Over the next two weeks our dear friends and book editors, Angela and Dan DePriest, cared for our family. With the help of food, movies, laughter, and love, we all rested and recuperated. Now, there was renewed hope for my survival.

I was still living in a pain-medication-induced fog. My appetite for both food and life was suppressed. I saw the world through black and white lenses. That troubled me. I stumbled aimlessly from bed to sofa and back to bed again each day, wondering if I would ever feel like my old self again.

My first trip out of the house came three weeks after surgery—a weekend woman's retreat with my church—my first pleasure outing in months. I not only had fun, but I got a taste of independence. I wanted more. So a week later I rented a car, drove to the hills of North Carolina, where I had grown up, and spent the next two weeks in a friend's condo atop scenic Sugar Mountain.

In the beginning, I thought this trip would be a chance for me to become self-sufficient again and finish writing this book, but it turned out to be so much

*more—a cathartic journey. Peter refers to it as my "mountaintop experience."
It was one of the most wonderful, yet difficult, adventures I've ever had.*

*I arrived at nine-thirty at night in a cloud of fog, after driving for hours
through torrential rains and heavy winds, all of which were quite a challenge
for me since I hadn't driven a car in months. At 5,000 feet, it was more winter
than spring and the winds were blowing a steady twenty to thirty miles per
hour, with gusts of up to fifty-five miles per hour. I was so grateful to finally
get inside, out of the cold rain. I couldn't wait to lie down. But the night clerk
put those thoughts out of my mind.*

*"We're supposed to get snow tonight . . . " the woman searched for my
room key. "They say about three to five inches."*

*"Really?" I suddenly realized I had no food. "Where's the nearest gro-
cery store?"*

"Oh, it's down the mountain, about three miles."

Out into the cold, sideways rain again. God help me . . . *Down the
foggy mountain.* I can't do this by myself. *Had to get groceries before the
store closed.* Oh, Lord, give me strength. *This was my introduction to in-
dependent living. Doing the shopping, cooking, and cleaning took everything
I had.*

*The first week was snowy and cold. The mountains, shrouded in fog,
seemed to match the cloudiness of my mind. Looking out the window was
like peering into my soul—dark and uncertain. I was tired most of the time,
but I made every effort to eat when I should and write when I could. I even
picked up my guitar a few times. But, the trauma of the last two years weighed
heavily on me.*

*I struggled with a sadness I could not put into words. Tears were
my only form of expression. Since I was all alone, I let the river run. At
night, the filtered light from the parking lot shone in through my bedroom window, casting shadows across the room. There in the quiet, I
lay in bed holding my hands to heaven and wailing in the dark. "Oh,
God," I cried. "Help me . . . " My arms reached higher. "Please . . . "
I begged. "Hold me." The sound of my hollow voice startled me and I tried to*

catch my breath, to pull myself together. But the tears continued. I wept from pain, I wept from loss. Anguish poured out of me in torrents, like a dam had broken in my soul and there was nothing I could do to stop it.

Then, finally, somewhere in the night, the tears subsided. I felt empty, as if there was nothing left in me. Not even breath. Was it possible to just stop breathing? *"Help me, God,"* I whispered. *"Help me . . . "*

I don't think a day went by that I didn't cry. But little by little, day by day, I began to feel my strength returning. Watching the icicles on my balcony melt, I felt the hope of spring.

By week two, the weather warmed and I began venturing outside, challenging myself to do a little walking. I worked up to a mile—it felt great to use my muscles again. Strolling alongside a mountain river and taking in the cool air was invigorating and I was reminded—I always find strength in the mountains.

One day, passing a brochure rack in a coffee shop, I picked up a pamphlet for Grandfather Mountain. Looking at the photo of the famous mile-high swinging bridge brought back a scene from my childhood: I was seven years old and the foster family I lived with was trying to make me cross that swinging bridge. Made of wood and cables, it wiggled precariously when people walked across it. I was terrified of falling. So I cried. They got angry. I cried harder. They threatened me. But I held my ground. Not a happy memory.

Suddenly, it came to me: Here's my chance to redo that scene. Grabbing my car keys, I headed out for Grandfather Mountain—I would cross that bridge when I came to it. Since it was right up the road, I figured it would take me about twenty minutes.

The afternoon sun cast a golden glow across the trees as I navigated the hairpin curves leading up to the mountain's 5,946-foot peak. Soon I was climbing the stairs leading up to the old suspension bridge. My heart raced—I could hardly wait to get there—it was almost in view.

But once at the top I stopped short. What happened? The old rickety bridge of long ago was gone; in its place, a new one, made of shiny galvanized steel, much sturdier. Not quite so scary. I stood there, pondering the significance *of this, noting how often my fear of doing something goes away once I summon the courage to "just do it."*

I stared at the bridge. Well, I thought, it's still a "mile high." I took a deep breath—time to face my fears, both old and new. Pulling out my cell phone, I took a picture of myself for posterity and stepped out on to the steely overpass. Safely on the other side, I climbed a few boulders, then stood atop a rocky ledge, taking in the spectacular view. I drew another deep breath. Somehow, I crossed over more than just a precarious bridge made of wood and metal. My conquered fear, the success of my new determination, buoyed my soul. I wanted to hold my arms up in the air and shout for joy, but there were people everywhere. Instead, I lifted my face to the heavens and thanked God. A moment I will never forget.

Days later, I took to the highway again—this time, to return home. I looked forward to joining my family for Easter Sunday dinner to celebrate the resurrection. Driving down the curvy roads, I noticed something happening— the cold, grey mountaintops were giving way to trees, surprisingly sprinkled with the warm green buds of spring. While I was sheltered up in the higher elevations, a new season had sprung down below.

The long winter had passed. My ongoing nightmare—running endlessly to escape the grasp of death's icy fingers—was over now. I'd awakened to the wonders of life stirring all around me. Daffodils and dogwoods were in bloom, the tender green of new grass and the blossoms of forsythia, known in the South as Yellow Bells—all hailed the arrival of spring. I rejoiced with them. Everything sparkled with intense clarity—the deep blue of the sky; the water-colored wonder of the foothills of Tennessee. The closer I got to home, the greener home became.

With each passing mile, I felt the fetters of the last two years fall away. I was truly free. And what's more, I understood I had always been free. Free to dream, to love, and live with all the passion God gave me. My heart, as it happens most days now, was filled with gratitude. I rolled down the car window, and started singing. Writing a song of my beloved mountains. And, for the first time in a long time, I dreamed of my future.

Before long, I was turning into our driveway. I glanced up into the rearview mirror to check my face, hardly recognizing the woman staring back at me. Had I really changed so much in just two weeks? *Maybe it was the lack of pain meds. Or maybe it was the realization I was actually going to make it. Just a few months ago, I was camped on death's doorstep. Now there was hope and fire in my eyes.*

Just then, the back door swung open. I broke into a smile as Peter and the girls ran out, eager to greet me. Crashing into one another, we hugged, laughed, and cried—all at the same time. Safe within their loving arms, I felt the hardships and pain of the past melting into memory.

I'd realized my mortality, climbed a mountain of fear, cried a river, and through the grace of God, come out on the other side of the darkest night of my soul. It felt like a miracle.

Standing in the golden glow of the late afternoon sun, holding my precious family, only one thought came to mind: It's great to be alive!

chapter 39

fire
walking

*Faith is taking the first step even when
you don't see the whole staircase.*

—Martn Luther King, Jr.

A s the Franklin traffic whizzed by, I made my way up to Calvin's of-fice. Almost three months out from surgery, I was feeling stronger every day. The stairs, once a challenge, were getting easier to climb. I was healing and each passing day was a step in the right direction.

It was good to see Calvin again after my long trip to the mountains. For the next thirty minutes, we talked about such subjects as the book, my trip, the changing season, and The Factory. Then I mentioned the BP oil spill that had happened down in the Gulf of Mexico. The oil rig that exploded and caused a terrible leak a month earlier was still not contained. Calvin was quiet and just shook his head. I should have known better. He never liked to focus on negative news. He changed the subject.

"I've always wondered . . . Where'd you get the name Stowe?"

"It's my middle name, from my great-great-grandmother, Lura Anne Stowe. I went by Anne for the first twenty or so years of my life, but I never really liked it . . . I didn't feel like an *Anne*, so I changed it to *Stowe*.

"And it's funny, how doing something as seemingly insignificant as changing my name really made a big difference in how I felt about myself."

He nodded. "Names—they're nothing more than labels. As soon as you label something you define its limitations. It's neither good nor bad, but you are defined by your name. Such as, my name is *Calvin Le-Hew*. I began forming an image of who that person was at a very early age and I associated limitations with my name."

"Like what?"

He ran his fingers back and forth across the top of the desk. "As a kid, I had an inferiority complex . . . I was short, and it shaped who I am. Over the years, I noticed how many short people become overachievers. I remember when I was a young page in the U.S. Senate . . . a short man came onto my elevator one day. I turned to him, 'Has anyone ever told you that you look like Harry Truman?'

"He put his arm right up here on my shoulder and with a smile, said, 'Son, I *am* Harry S. Truman!' "

I laughed.

Calvin's voice dropped. "I was staggered at how short he was . . . but later, while studying what makes people successful, I found that there are a lot of short people who make it big . . . to overcome the poor self image caused by that label."

"Mmm, I've noticed that too. There seem to be a lot of movie stars—especially men—who are short."

"Yes, but they rise above that. They *create* the image of who they want to be." Calvin was in his element now, using his hands, teaching. "You can't judge people, or even things, necessarily by appearance . . . For instance, when I returned to Franklin years ago, there were seven old vacant buildings. At least, that's probably how they *appeared* to most people. But I always try to see *what things can be*, and not *what they seem to be*. I saw them as successful businesses. So, whether it's something material, a relationship or our own image . . . we create these things.

"In the Bible you see the words, I AM. This is the name of the Creator. Whatever you put behind the words I AM is a definition of what you create for yourself. Like, I AM a poor speller. I AM a talented individual. Or, I AM a child of God. It changes your perception of yourself, which changes your behavior, which changes everything in your life.

"I think it's important to see yourself as a winner. That doesn't mean you have to become egotistical. But your self-image will determine what you create for yourself. Give up the old self! The Bible says, 'Be ye transformed by the renewing of your mind.'

"Whether you know it or not, you are a born winner . . . " His eyes narrowed and his lips crept up mischievously. "What if I told you that you were going to be in a race with a hundred thousand other people?

"Uh . . . I think I'd panic. "

"And what if I said you would be the winner?"

I laughed aloud. "I'd say 'You're kidding!'"

"No, I'm not." He held his hand out toward me. "Before you were born, your mother and father got together to conceive you. And guess what? *You* won the great sperm race! Going *uphill!* You were *born* a winner!"

"Hmm. I never thought of it like that."

"We're all born winners. The only thing holding back any of us are the limitations we put on ourselves by the choices we make . . . It's our self-talk that gets us down. Our subconscious is so powerful—it's always listening. What you think about, you bring about. But that's where we're very fortunate. We can always reprogram our minds . . . that's what people who walk on hot coals do . . . "

"Yes, I remember you mentioning that. Tell me about it."

Calvin leaned back. "Well, I'll tell you, stepping out on hot coals is literally stepping out on faith—you have to believe you can do it. It's risky, yes. But over and over in the Bible you see people taking risks, stepping out on faith. I guess I just had to try it and see if I could do it."

"So—what happened?"

"Well, it all started when I heard about the Aborigines walking on coals and I thought, *I'd like to learn more about that.* Then I met a lady at church who'd done fire walking and, you know, it's always easier to do something when you know someone who's done it. So I flew out to San Diego where Tony Robbins was teaching a fire-walking class.

"At first I thought it was an illusion. Maybe they were hypnotized. Or maybe they were padding their feet with something before walking on the coals. But it wasn't anything like that at all. Tony trained us—using something called 'neuro-linguistic programming.'

"What's that?"

"Tony called it 'anchoring.' On the first night, after about two hours of teaching, we laid down on the floor and got into a meditative state. Then Tony said, 'Try to think of every experience in which you were a winner, even back when you were in grammar school and the teacher praised one of your drawings. Every time you remember something, clench your fist. For every success you've had, clench your fist so you can really *feel* it.'"

Calvin held out his left arm and rubbed it. "I still get chill-bumps every time I do that, because the programming to my subconscious is activated. I get that winning feeling."

By now, I knew a lot about Calvin's talent for visualization. I wondered if that technique would work for me, so I tried clenching my fist, thinking of times when I was a winner. I made a mental note to try this again at home.

"Next," Calvin continued, "he told us to visualize ourselves going across the coals, keeping our heads up as we walked. That was the whole point—to not 'look down' in life—always look up. And he also instructed us to walk at a normal pace. He didn't want us to stumble or fall.

"So we took off our shoes and socks, rolled up our pant legs, and headed out toward the coals. I'll never forget seeing them as I turned the corner. It was like an evening barbeque. You could see the flames and sparks—that's how hot they were."

"Were you scared?"

"Oh my gosh, yes. I thought, *This is real! I can't do this . . .* "

"How'd you get past the fear?"

"I really wanted to do it . . . so I just marched myself up to the front of the line. That way, I couldn't talk myself out of it."

"You've got guts."

He shook his head. "Most people talk themselves out of the things they fear. They start rationalizing why they *can't* do something. Why they *shouldn't* do it. I wanted to get beyond that negative self-talk. So after I saw Tony Robbins do it, I thought, *Okay, a human being walked across the coals—it can be done.*

"And just before we went he told us to visualize cool moss, to say to ourselves while walking across, *cool moss, cool moss . . .* "

"So . . . how did it feel?"

Calvin leaned back. "It was unbelievable, Stowe! I could actually feel the coals crunching between my toes. You can't believe how hot they were. But there was no pain! It was like walking through crunching ice.

"And once we got across, there was some water to walk through just in case we had any coals stuck between our toes. Afterwards, I couldn't believe I'd really done it. I went back and tried to pick up one of the coals—"

"You didn't—"

"Yes, I did. I just wanted to see if it was really that hot. But I couldn't even get close. And then a funny thing happened . . . after about thirty minutes, blisters began forming on my feet. They were so painful! When we got back to the conference room, Tony asked if anyone had blisters. There were about seven out of a hundred who raised their hand. He explained that it was probably because we wanted to prove to ourselves that it really was as hot as we thought—that it was no illusion.

"Then he suggested that we put our hand over here under our armpit and just pull back. It had something to do with the lymph system, which somehow made sense, scientifically. He said we'd feel no pain in the morning."

"Really?"

"That's what he told us . . . So, the next morning I got up, not thinking anything about it. All of a sudden I was conscious of my feet and I thought, *Oh, I'm walking!* There were no blisters. They didn't hurt at all!"

"Unbelievable."

"Well, believe it or not, this is the power of the subconscious. Call it suggestion or whatever. It worked. The 'cool moss' and the suggestion for relieving the pain . . . we accepted as truth. And maybe, like a placebo, it worked because I *believed* it would work. Back when I owned the drugstores, our pharmacist told me how many of the prescriptions he actually filled with placebos. But they worked because the patient believed the doctor. Again, our minds and the words we say are just so powerful."

We sat in silence for a moment. The fire-walking story was amazing. But what impressed me was the message about the *power of our words* . . .

Something amusing had happened just the day before. I thought Calvin might get a kick out of it so I told him the story.

"Peter and I had just finished watching a DVD when I commented on the poor picture quality and advanced age of our television. I remember saying it was 'out-of-date' and an 'antique.' It was the second time in twenty-four hours I'd talked despairingly about it. The words were barely out of my mouth when, all of a sudden, we heard a loud *pop* from the TV, followed by a high whining sound. An acrid smell wafted through the room and, thinking the TV was on fire, we quickly carried it outside."

I made a face and shook my head. "It's sitting on the back porch now . . . a goner."

Calvin broke into a smile, his eyes disappearing into crinkles.

"Ha!" He laughed. You better watch what you say, Stowe! Your words *are* powerful!"

chapter 40

lessons from
the factory

*Whether you think you can or can't,
either way you are right.*

—Henry Ford

On Saturday morning, with the breezes of early summer blowing, I pulled into The Factory and stepped through the glass door of Building 2, an office I rarely go in. Taking the elevator upstairs, I entered into a beautifully wood-paneled oval conference room, formerly the spacious offices of Pioneer Music. Big Idea, the company that produces Veggie Tales animations, is on the floor below. Companies like these make Building 2 a hotbed of creative energy. Today, Peter tapped into that energy to shoot a video of Calvin giving a PowerPoint presentation, complete with pictures and a quick tour of his life story.

I glanced around at the small audience gathering to hear one of Franklin's most prominent citizens speak, then I took a seat. In the back of the room, the cameras were ready. In the front, Peter helped Calvin pin on his microphone.

Three, two, one . . . rolling.

Moments later, Calvin recounted his life story for a mesmerized audience. They listened as he told them about his worst day, and his life in Washington, D.C., the Tallahassee drugstores, and the Ten Brave Christians, Carter's Court, California, Choices, and all the scenic stories along the way. Once again, I realized I was listening to a consummate storyteller and teacher.

This, aside from all the real estate, money making, and business success, is one of Calvin's greatest passions. He loves to, as he puts it, "teach people how to fish." All the money and recognition he gained was a little "boring." I'd heard him use that word to describe material success more than once . . . His greatest passion now is helping other people raise their consciousness, to live up to their own greatest purposes, potentials, and God-given gifts. It seemed that, along the way, Calvin had also found another of his own great gifts and purposes.

Most of the first half of his seminar was familiar to me, but about midway through he began speaking about our feelings as *vibrations*. He had my attention.

"I used to think it was all in my head . . . in my brain, between here and here," He put one hand on the top of his head, the other under his chin. "But I've since added the heart to that equation." He lowered one hand to his chest. "Science is even *showing* us that the heart gives off energy. It creates something like an electromagnetic field of attraction.

"Many times in life," he said, "you'll think of somebody and the phone will ring and it's them. This is thought transfer. Our thoughts send out vibrations, or energy . . . You might have heard the expression, 'What you think about, you bring about.' This is so powerful. But how does that work? It works because of what some call the *Law of Attraction*.

"The Law of Attraction says, 'that which is like unto itself is drawn.' It's similar to the Golden Rule—do unto others as you would have them do unto you. The vibrations of our thoughts literally attract what we desire into our lives. For example, when you want to listen to a particular radio station, say 98.9, you turn the dial to 98.9. You don't tune the dial to 107.2—that would only bring static. You align to the matching frequency of the station you wish to listen to. In the same way, we must also be in tune with the desires of our heart.

"That's where paying attention to our emotions pays off. Our emotions are a sure sign of how our thoughts are vibrating. When you are focused on something you want, something you desire, you feel wonderful, right? When you're focused on something you don't desire, you feel awful. Your emotions, then, are a barometer for your vibrations. Good or bad—we draw to ourselves that which we feel most strongly about. Dreams can come true. However, it requires being consistent and deliberate in your thoughts, by creating a vibrational harmony with your desires. The easiest way to bring about vibrational harmony is to do like Jesus says: ' . . . whatever you ask for in prayer—in your heart—*believe that you have received it*, and it will be yours.'

"When there is something you desire you must keep your thoughts and feelings—your vibrations—in alignment. Focusing on the *lack* of that which you desire will bring only feelings of anger, worry, or discouragement. On the other hand, thoughts that are *in line* with what you desire will bring about feelings of excitement, joy, gratitude, and anticipation. That's where you want to be."

Vibratory energy. Calvin and I often talked about vibrational medicine, which interested both of us. I was diagnosed with CT scans and PET scans using radiographic frequencies and treated with several alternative cancer methods using a variety of spectral frequencies, electrical vibrations, and other pseudo-scientific-sounding methods. But this was the first time I'd thought about the body or mind actually *sending out* frequencies. I considered my journey through cancer and wondered if my own negative vibrations had played a part in my sickness. While I was pondering that, Calvin shifted gears. Now he was talking about The Factory.

"So, how did I end up with The Factory?" He crossed his arms over his chest. "Well, it started when I got a call from Mary Pierce, the head of the Heritage Foundation. She said, 'Calvin, we've got a problem. The city of Franklin is talking about leasing the old Stoveworks Factory to a film company for a movie scene . . . They want to blow it up!'

"It's hard to believe," Calvin stretched out his hands, "but the whole place, including this building we're in right now, was for sale for $650,000. Forty-six acres. Three hundred thousand square feet under one roof. But it was all dilapidated, in bad shape with decay, asbestos, underground storage tanks—lots of problems. Nobody seemed to want it. The mayor called it a white elephant.

"That's why Mary called me. She said, 'Calvin, we can't let them blow it up . . . ' Now, it wasn't a big historical monument. It didn't have that much character. But it had, at one time, been the largest employer for the people of Williamson County. There was so much potential . . . and I love saving old buildings . . . so off I went.

"Some of you may know Wynonna Judd, the singer. She used to be a waitress at Miss Daisy's Tea Room, and we got to be friends with her family. Well, I remembered Wynonna telling me one time that she wanted to do something for the youth of Williamson County—she wanted to get them off the streets, to build them a place where they could play basketball and do things. I thought, *That's a great idea!* So I called her and gave her and Naomi and Larry, their manager, a tour. They liked it—but it didn't work out.

"So I called a few other people from Nashville who had the means to buy it. I told them, 'This place has so much value . . . and they're only asking $650,000 for all of it.' Well, every time I showed it I could see the potential. I saw the steel I-beams. I saw the millions of bricks, worth 12-1/2 cents each. We'd done Carter's Court, we renovated old houses and buildings, and I thought, *Why not?*" Calvin paused, offering an outstretched arm toward his wife, Marilyn, who was in the audience. "Fortunately, I'm married to a wonderful lady. We've been through it all together. But she must've seen it coming and thought, *Here we go again . . .*"

Everyone turned toward Marilyn for a moment. She shook her head, gesturing for Calvin to go on.

"So we went to the mayor," Calvin continued, "and told him we'd pay $650,000 for it. But he said, 'In order to make it legal we're going to have to receive a sealed bid. So, they advertised in the paper and we met one night down at city hall. There were two other bidders. By this time, I *really* wanted it . . . so I bid one million dollars. And I got it.

"Then I found out I couldn't get financing. There were so many negatives we had to overcome. Chemicals, underground storage tanks, and so on. Negatives—we all have them in our lives.

"If I had known beforehand that renovating the electricity in the main building and Jamison Hall alone would cost over $600,000, I'm not sure I would have gone through with it." Calvin tapped his fingers together, then seized the moment for a lesson . . . "Sometimes, we're better off not knowing how long or costly the journey is going to be. Otherwise, we'd never venture anywhere at all. Yes, we overcame a lot of hurdles, we spent a lot of money—about a million dollars just cleaning up the place—getting it safe and sound. Like life—there were negatives and problems—but we can always rise above."

As Calvin talked, I had a hard time relating to the massive scope of these kinds of problems, yet I knew, on some level, I needed that same positive attitude to overcome my own day-to-day trials.

"So, for me," he said, "it's a kind of exciting to be here today, after all we've been through. Today, at The Factory, we have 73 tenants, good tenants. And every one of the businesses are either artistic, creative, unique, musical, or food related.

Calvin held out his arms. "This 12,000-square-foot space we're in now is soon going to be the Nashville Film Institute. We're surrounded by creative people. We've set up a consciousness here. And it's the law of attraction that draws in like-minded people and businesses.

"But that attraction isn't just between people . . . buildings and entire towns can exude a consciousness or vibe that attracts others. It's one of the reasons why Leipers Fork, my old stomping grounds, is such a great place now. People love being there. They like the atmosphere. A lot of music stars have moved into Leipers Fork and they've set up their own consciousness—they don't want subdivisions there. And it's working.

"Here at The Factory, we've set up a consciousness of artists and creative people. Now, they're very right-brained kind of people . . . " Calvin raised his eyebrows. "Sometimes I wish they were more left-brained, in order to make the rent come more often . . . "

The audience laughed.

"But it's worked out. We've all done well. Ignorance is bliss sometimes. It takes a crazy person to do the things I've done . . . I've given a lot of credit to my low IQ—it gets me into some things I might not have gotten into otherwise." He held up his finger. "But when you keep the faith and believe, it works.

"Before we end our program, I want to share with you something I developed for a book I wrote called *Manifesting Dreams*." Calvin hit the advance button on his laptop, beginning a series of PowerPoint images. "I call these 'The Seven Steps to Achievement.' I think they sum up much of what I learned about accomplishing what you want in life."

The audience watched as an animated graphic of a bright red ladder appeared on the screen. Bullet points coincided with each of the seven rungs of the ladder and Calvin read them aloud.

1. DESIRE – Here's where it starts. You want something that is not presently with you . . . it has to be achieved.

2. IMAGE – You must form a *mental* image of that thing or situation, which you desire—whether it's a visible thing like a new car or an invisible thing like love.

3. GOAL – The image and the goal actually overlap. After you desire something, you form an image of it in your mind's eye and then set it as a goal. Writing it down is important. Refer back to it often.

4. FAITH AND BELIEF – Those two key words again. The Bible has much to say about faith and belief: *According to your faith will it be done unto you.* And you must believe that you will have what you desire. Like I said earlier, *Believe that you have received it, and it will be yours.*

5. ACT – This is the most important step. Most people stop here. *Taking action gets you out of your comfort zone.* Once you set your goal and hold that image before you, you must willfully *step out in faith.*

6. GIVE – You must give in order to receive. This is a Law of the Universe. In business, you have to give a product or service in order to receive compensation. Likewise, if you want love, you must give love.

7. RECEIVE – There must be no feeling of guilt or unworthiness. If so, there must be forgiveness—either for you or toward others. You must have a good self-image, or you will unconsciously sabotage your goals."

After reading each point, Calvin kept his eyes on the screen and, like any good teacher, went back over it, expanding on his message. He recently shared with me his philosophy of teaching: "Tell 'em what you're going to tell 'em. Tell 'em. Then tell 'em what you told 'em."

"Regarding the fifth step," he said, "Action is what people are often missing. I think many people in New Age or New Thought philosophy miss this very important step. They think they can get in the lotus position and meditate and just find gold in their hand. I haven't discovered that yet. You have to put ideas into action.

"With steps number six and seven, you really do have to GIVE in order to RECEIVE. I don't know why they didn't teach this in the business schools at University of Tennessee or George Washington University where I majored in economics, but that ought to be taught like a law of business. What is the Golden Rule? Do unto others as you would have them do unto you. Treat others how you'd like to be treated. If you want money—and most people do—it is by giving people either a product or a service. The most successful business on Main Street is the one that gives the most. That is the law."

Calvin leaned back in his chair and surveyed the room. "The whole point of this program is that *you can do things you don't ordinarily think you can do.* There is a power greater than we are that is available to help us.

"I'd like to finish with a quote from the greatest teacher who ever walked the face of the earth." He pressed the last key on his Power-Point presentation, and the final slide faded up slowly.

I tell you the truth, anyone who has faith in me
will do what I have been doing.
He will do even greater things than these,
because I am going to the Father.

– JESUS CHRIST

A crowd of people left The Factory that day, some with new-found knowledge, some with reinforcements for what they already knew. One thing was certain, though; no one left empty-handed. As for me, it didn't matter that Calvin had just spoken to a room filled with people—it felt like his message was just for me.

may 18, 2010

*T*ODAY IS MY BIRTHDAY. *I cannot remember, for the life of me, a time when I have felt happier to celebrate this particular day. What makes this year so special is the birthday present I'm getting—life.*

Of course, I realize I've been receiving this same gift for all of my forty-nine years but, somehow, today it feels different. After having almost lost it I feel, now more than ever, how precious it is.

I have been given yet another chance to reach out to someone in need; to make amends to those I've hurt; to say, "I love you;" and to sing the song in my heart. I'm especially thankful for these opportunities, for I know firsthand that we don't always get so lucky. For instance, when we say to one another, "See you tomorrow," it's only a wish, a hope that we will be together again, not a promise.

I had an experience last year that drove this point home to me in an unforgettable way. It haunted me for weeks and it's a lesson I keep close to my heart. This is a true story. It became a song.

*It was spring 2009 and my sister-in-law, Christine, and her two daugh-
ters were in town for a visit. "Hey, Stowe," Christine said. "Know anywhere
we can we go to hear some live music?"*

*"Live music?" I thought for a moment. Strangely enough, even though
we live near Nashville, Tennessee—commonly referred to as Music City—
there weren't a lot of places to hear live music. But since I'd been singing at a
writer's night recently, I knew of one. "Sure. I'll take you to The Frisky Berry,
up at The Factory."*

*A few hours later we stood just outside the door of The Frisky Berry. As
I listened to the strains of a singer-songwriter from inside the café, I noticed
how different the atmosphere of The Factory is at night. During the day, there
are plenty of overhead windows to light the place. At night, with the lamps
along the hallway, it resembles a small city street from long ago, warm and
inviting.*

*We walked into the coffee shop, ordered some tea, and searched around
for a seat. I ended up on a sofa directly in front of the stage. A great
spot. I leaned back into the cushy pillows to enjoy the music of a talented
young lady.*

*Almost immediately, a tall middle-aged man with long black hair sat
down beside me. "Hi," he smiled. "I'm Gregg."*

*"Nice to meet you," I said quietly, not wanting to disturb
the singer. I nodded to Gregg and turned my attention back to
the stage.*

*But he was persistent. He leaned into me, "I sang a little earlier in the
evening."*

"Oh. Sorry I missed you."

*"Well, I sing here almost every Thursday . . ." he brushed the hair out
of his eyes, "usually around seven-thirty."*

*"Great! I'm singing here next week. Maybe I'll come a little early and
see you."*

*"You're a singer too?" He broke into a wide grin. "Man, I'd really like
to sing a song for you." He tilted his head up, as if devising a plan. "I'm*

gonna go ask the manager if he'll let me do another one." And just like that, he was gone.

Wow, this guy really has a passion for his music. *Watching him talk his way into another performance, I couldn't help but wonder,* Where does that kind of drive come from? *I loved singing and entertaining others, but I was always cautious about pushing it on anyone—I didn't want to seem like I was tooting my own horn. Yet, if recent events of my life had taught me anything, it's that time waits for no one. Lately, there was an old saying that haunted me, a broken record echoing in my head—"Don't die with your song still in your heart."*

A few minutes later, Gregg returned, triumphant. "Okay . . . " he pulled out his guitar. "Rich says I can go on after the last songwriter."

"Really?" I looked at my watch, then back at my nieces. One of them, Ani, was already leaning on her mother. I turned back to Gregg. "Mmm, I don't know if my family's going to hold out 'til then . . . I might have to wait 'til next week."

"Ahh, no," he grabbed my arm. "Please, don't leave. I'm going to sing U2's, I Still Haven't Found What I'm Looking For.*"*

"That's amazing! I was just studying those lyrics this morning. I'd love to hear you sing it . . . but . . . " I gave him a tight smile. "We'll see."

A few songs later, as expected, Christine tapped me on the shoulder. "We need to head out, Stowe. The kids are falling asleep."

I nodded and leaned over to Gregg. "My sister-in-law is ready to go."

He looked like a little boy who'd just lost his puppy. "Don't leave," he pleaded.

"Look," I gave him my best consolation smile. "I'll see you next week . . . okay? Seven-thirty."

"Yeah . . . sure." He mumbled. "See you."

I felt bad for the guy, but I took comfort knowing I would make it up to him next Thursday. He could sing for me then.

The next week, I arrived promptly at seven-thirty. Walking in the door,

I noticed a girl on stage singing a ballad. Hmm, I wonder where he is? I waited through a few more songs.

Then Rich, the owner of The Frisky Berry, took the microphone. He rubbed his forehead nervously. "Uhm . . . " his voice trembled, "this evening, a dear friend of ours, Gregg Fulkerson, was supposed to be here . . . but he's . . . he couldn't be with us. Gregg . . . died this past Tuesday of a brain aneurism."

An audible gasp rose from the audience. I stood, drop-jawed, taking in the news. Was he talking about the guy I met last week?

"Gregg," he continued, "will be forever remembered for the songs he wrote . . . he loved to sing . . . Next week we're going to have a memorial service here for him. We'll sing some of his songs . . . I hope you all can come."

The rest of the evening was a blur. I performed a thirty-minute set but I don't recall much about it. I just couldn't believe Gregg was gone. And I never got to hear him sing.

For days, I kept my guitar close by. There was something brewing in me—a song that wanted to be birthed. I tried several different versions but nothing sounded right. I found myself lying awake nights, thinking about what had happened and wondering how I could express it in a song. I'd hoped to sing at the memorial service, but it was almost Thursday and so far I'd come up empty. Sitting on my bed on Wednesday afternoon, I strummed a few chords. How could I honor Gregg? I was just about to lay it down when it came to me; just tell the story.

The next evening, I took the stage. It was Thursday, the night when Gregg usually sang. He wasn't there, of course. Instead, I was sitting on the stool where he usually sat, looking out across the audience he usually sang to, most of whom were his friends.

"I didn't know him well . . . " I began. "But in those few moments we were together, one thing was clear; all he wanted to do was sing. He wanted to sing his song . . . for me. Unfortunately, he didn't get that chance. So I *am here tonight in his place. And if you don't mind, I'd like to sing my song for you."*

———⊗⊗⊗———

Song For You

'Bout a week ago last Thursday
At a café down the street
Met a guy who played the guitar
When he sat down next to me
Didn't feel too much like talking
So I just listened with a smile
He said I'd like to play you something
Could you stick around a while

Chorus:
Let me sing my song for you
It's the only thing in this world
That I know how to do
And sometimes when I'm feeling low
It's all that gets me through
Let me sing my song for you

I said I'm with some other folks
But I'll stay if I can
He said I've been a bit down on my luck
But I used to have a band
Now it's writer's nights on Thursdays
7:30 until 8:00
Well how 'bout I see you next week
He grabbed me and said wait

(Chorus)

Why dance we not why stand we still [vii]
I've often wondered this
We never get a second chance
For moments that we miss

I went to see him sing last Thursday
But the stage lights were all low
And the manager grew misty-eyed
As he took the microphone
He said we lost a good friend the other day
Oh, he took his final bow
So if you're out there somewhere
I hope you can hear me now

(Chorus)

chapter 42

a light in
the darkness

*The Light shines in the darkness and the darkness
can never extinguish it.*

—JOHN 1:5

I walked across the parking lot, past the beautiful bubbling fountain
and ornamental trees and plants just outside The Factory. The old
building, with its rugged brick façade, stood before me and I paused for
just a moment in its shadow, enjoying the cool shade. With the book
almost finished I found myself wondering what would become of our
Monday morning meetings.

Once inside, I greeted Gerry, the receptionist, and headed up
the steps to Calvin's office. I felt strong as I climbed higher, each
step reminding me of how far I'd come since my operation in February. I was really on the upswing now and looking forward to my time
with Calvin.

"Mornin!" I knocked on the door.

"Come on in!" came the familiar refrain.

We hugged, as usual, then settled into our chairs. Almost immediately, I noticed a quietness about Calvin.

"You doing okay?"

"Yes . . . " he shrugged. "A little low energy maybe."

"Hmm . . . " I tried to hide my concern. "What do you think is causing it?"

He shifted in his seat. "I don't know, Stowe . . . it started around the time I found out I had cancer. It comes and goes."

He sighed. "It reminds me of my analogy of the tripod—the physical, mental, and spiritual balancing act we all do . . . "

"Yes . . . "

"It's well known that mental or emotional stress can lead to physical sickness, like hypertension and heart attacks . . . even cancer."

"Do you think your cancer was stress-related?"

"Absolutely. I'm sure that's what happened to me a few years ago. I was so out of balance that my body began to topple. And I think in the same way that emotional stress can lead to physical illnesses, physical ailments can cause emotional problems."

"Like depression?"

He nodded. "Like depression."

"I know you've struggled with that . . . " I studied his face. "Do you mind talking about it?"

Calvin pushed his bottom lip up and took a deep breath. "You know, this has been a tough one for me to face . . . I mean, here we are writing a book about the power of positive thinking, and I'm dealing with depression every day. It makes me think, 'Who am I to be offering advice?'" He lowered his eyes.

"Someone who faces his fears head-on?"

He raised his head and gave a half-smile.

"So, do you think the depression is a result of the cancer?"

"I'd say there was probably a correlation there, but I didn't realize I was in a depression until I got to where . . . I'd wake up and not want to do anything, not even get out of bed. I really just didn't want to live." Calvin's face tightened, as if in pain. "I had to overcome that. Psychiatrists gave me all kinds of pills . . . I tried some alternative treatments.

Nothing seemed to do any good. Finally, I just quit all of those things. I became quiet. I went inward."

I thought about the progression of the things he'd listed—the emotional stress led to physical illness, the treatment of that illness led to depression and, finally, the depression made him look inward. In the process he'd become vulnerable. I related to it as a form of mourning. When someone goes through a life-changing illness or accident, there is a feeling of loss for the person they used to be, the life they used to have. Grief is the natural consequence. It's painful. It empties your heart. But in that space of emptiness, if you remain open, it is an opportunity to be filled with God's comfort.

I cleared my throat. "Do you think it was your body's way of getting your mind and spirit to do that very thing—to go inward?"

"It's possible. Cancer was definitely a signal for me to slow down. Or, maybe, to wake up to life. I'm actually glad I went through it." Calvin rubbed a hand on the back of his neck. "I don't know about the depression though. If I could only be aware and conscious of all the mishaps I've gone through, without being depressed . . . " He fixed his eyes out the window, as a noisy truck pulled up outside. "For me, it always comes back to looking for that 'seed of greatness.'"

I lifted my eyebrows. "Have you found any seeds of greatness in depression?"

Calvin shook his head. "To be honest with you, Stowe, I really don't know. It's definitely a dark place in anybody's life when they go through this kind of sadness . . . " He held his hands out, palms up. "But I also have to believe 'This too shall pass.'

"Something that helps is doing things for other people . . . like what we're doing here now, writing this book. It allows me to get away from myself personally, and away from thinking about my own health problems. This is good for me. And it's the only goal and desire I have right now. I really don't care much about the material things, or ego-centered parts of life anymore."

"I know what you mean, Calvin. Losing my health was a great wake up call for me too. I've always heard if you don't have your health, nothing else matters. Money, fame, whatever—they don't mean a thing if you're stuck in bed and in pain."

"Yes . . . "

"And I'm so grateful to be healing now," I said. "I'm getting my appetite back . . . and not just for food. I feel more excited about living than I ever have. It's given me a whole new perspective."

"Yes, I can see that." Calvin smiled. "It's like soaring above it all after being so low. You've got a new viewpoint on life. Your tripod—the spiritual, mental, and physical—is balanced." Calvin took a sip of water. "For me, I can see that my spiritual leg was always the shortest. But whenever I became aware of being uneven, I visualized my tripod rebalanced . . . and more than just for myself. I prayed for and visualized my family and other people becoming balanced too. It made me conscious of doing for others, including animals."

"There's something about serving others that makes you feel alive, doesn't it?"

Calvin agreed. "It's hard to explain how good it feels . . . But it comes when you devote yourself to loving others, to creating something in your life that gives you purpose and meaning. And when you're sincere, when it really comes from the heart, I think it's a pure connection to God."

"A way of growing the spiritual leg of your tripod?"

"Yes," he said. "I remember in the Ten Brave Christian group, when I first became conscious of serving others—helping someone, making them smile when they're down, giving them hope—all of that made me feel so good. I was proud of myself, but it wasn't from an ego place. And it was a major way of working on that spiritual leg. It's the *little things* we do . . . they mean a lot more than we realize."

"The little things . . . " That expression took me back a few years. "It reminds me of when Peter made the *Life After Life* film about near-death experiences . . . people talked about how God's Light pointed out the spiritually important parts of the life they'd just experienced. And it was always the 'little things' they did for people that seemed to make the biggest difference in God's view."

"I believe that . . . " He said. "And maybe gaining empathy from hardships helps us find compassion for others. I read something just this morning about adversity and crisis." Calvin touched two fingers to his lips and began searching his desk. "Now let me see . . . Ah," he picked up a book. "Here it is. *The Power of Coincidence: How Life Shows Us What We Need to Know.*" He opened to a bookmarked page and began reading: "'Without suffering, I would never have found my inner resources. Never have felt the grief that gives me depth and character. Never have opened my heart to compassion.'" [viii]

Calvin looked up for a moment, as if savoring the message, then continued. "'Crisis usually represents a confrontation or an argument with one or more of the conditions of existence. Crisis is a challenge to change. To change is to locate a new level of strength in ourselves, and to act in accord with it. To stay unchanged is to regress. There is no middle ground of safety. This is why in crisis we enter the void. We see how much of our security was a prop, meant to uphold a shaky ego. In crisis, we feel powerless to maintain the old comfortable structures. We are then forced to marshal our strengths and move into something new. Perhaps a grace comes our way. We find strength we did not think we had. We live through the crisis. We are still standing after the storm. What threatens us with breakdown, leads to breakthrough.'" [ix]

Calvin laid the book down. He looked peaceful.

"So . . . " I said, "thank God for a crisis?"

"Yes," he smiled. "Thank God."

increasing awareness

All men should learn before they die,
what they are running from, and to, and why.

—James Thurber

Back in the 18th century a French philosopher, Blaise Pascal, talked about a modern metaphor for the yearning of the soul—what drives us on our spiritual quest. He wrote, "There is a God-shaped hole in the heart of every man which cannot be filled by any created thing, but only by God the Creator."

I recalled the "God-shaped hole" quote one day while sitting in the big Queen Anne chair in Calvin's office. He and I were discussing our spiritual journeys—where we'd come from, where we were going. Calvin brought up my song, *Second Chance*, and how a life crisis slows a person down, giving them a second chance to rethink what matters, what they're really searching for. We have a tendency, in the busyness of life, to overlook our innate longing to simply connect with our Creator.

"It's natural," Calvin said, "to try and fill that void inside us with all kinds of things—work, sex, alcohol, TV, our family, whatever. None of that really satisfies us though."

I nodded.

"I mean, take me, for example." Calvin held out his hands. "I've tried it all, zigzagging from one thing to another; a millionaire, a speaker, a preservationist, a pilot . . . yet deep down inside my desire has been to live a 'life that really matters.' I want to connect, like Pascal says, with my Creator."

I glanced up at an airplane model, then back at Calvin. "You want to fly higher . . . "

"Always . . . I did a seminar back in 1986." Calvin tapped his fingers on a cassette tape lying off to one side of his desk. "I listened to it the other day, just for fun . . . I was just beginning to deal with the idea of evolving consciousness."

"What was it about?"

"You ever hear in developmental psychology about Maslow's Hierarchy of Needs?"

"It sounds familiar, but it's been a while . . . "

"Well, Maslow wrote that our basic physical needs are food, water, sleep, and sex. Once those are satisfied, we need physical security, not just for our bodies, but also for our family, our health, and our possessions. Next, we need love and a sense of belonging from those around us. Beyond that, there's the need for self-esteem, achievement, confidence, and mutual respect with others. And, finally, there's the need for self-actualization—a fulfillment of our need for creativity, morality, spontaneity, open-mindedness, and the ability to objectively solve problems. There's an inborn desire to develop into self-actualization, and Maslow said, 'What a man can be, he must be.' So as we go through a personal evolution or development—even through a crisis like cancer—we tend to get beyond the ego and the need for materialism."

"Mmm."

"You ever hear of Ken Keyes?

"No."

"He was another guy who really studied consciousness and awareness. He developed what he called the 'seven centers of consciousness.'

It was kind of similar to Maslow's but even more spiritual. For years, I've vacillated up and down all of these centers.

"The first level is what he called 'The Security Center.' This is where you are dominated by thoughts of food and shelter. Things. Your mind is preoccupied by the idea of 'getting enough.' Getting enough sleep, getting enough money . . . getting, getting.

"The next level of consciousness is the 'Sensation Center,' where we receive pleasure. We try to find happiness in these sensations—the taste of food, sex, the sounds of music, and so on. None of these things should be labeled as wrong . . . they're part of our human experience. But the key is awareness. Consciously or unconsciously choosing where we want to be on this level.

"The next center is the 'Power Center' . . . this is where the Donald Trumps of the world live . . . dominating people and situations, increasing prestige, wealth, and pride.

"Then there is the 'Love Center.' You see yourself in everyone. You feel compassion for those who are suffering and you begin to accept and love everyone unconditionally, even yourself. That's a biggie; loving yourself . . . I've had a hard time with that one."

"Me, too."

"Next," he continued, "is the 'Cornucopia Center.' You're able to see a perfect world more often. You reprogram your addictions and become more accepting, loving, and generous. 'Your cup runneth over' because you see the world as a 'horn of plenty.'

"Then there is the 'Conscious Awareness Center.' He also called it being 'an observer.' Here, you see yourself and others play the games from the previous levels. You rid yourself of fear. It is a place of peace when all around you things are falling apart. The person who can stay calm and not lose his cool remains at this center . . . sort of like Benjamin Franklin, when his experimental lab was burning. As he stood there in the middle of the night watching it burn, someone said, 'Oh Mr. Franklin, how terrible . . . '

"Ben just observed the fire quietly, then said, 'Well, the flames are beautiful!' He had that type of consciousness about him. He could see something positive about it.

"Finally, there is what Keys calls 'Cosmic Consciousness.' Some people refer to it as 'Christ Consciousness.' Here, you transcend self-awareness and become pure awareness or consciousness. You are one with all and everything. You are love, peace, beauty, wisdom, and oneness."

"So how would you suggest we get to these states?"

"Well, I used to think it was with our thoughts." He tapped his forehead with his index finger. "But our thoughts are up here. To achieve 'Christ Consciousness' the idea has to make the journey to here." Calvin lowered his hand to his heart. "Jesus says, *If anyone says to this mountain, 'Go throw yourself into the sea, and does not doubt in his heart but believes what he says will happen, it will be done for him.'* That means that in order to achieve the kind of Christ Consciousness Jesus embodied, we must pray through our heart and believe that it is done."

He looked into my eyes. "That's really hard for me sometimes because I have the tendency to think I can read or work my way to that kind of consciousness . . . but I know it's not a mental thing . . . it's how open we are to the Spirit."

"It's about connecting, isn't it?"

"Yes." He said. "Our greatest need—maybe even our greatest purpose—is to reconnect to the heart of God . . . St. Augustine knew that. He wrote, 'You have made us for yourself, O Lord, and our heart is restless until it rests in You.' And the way we become aware of the infinite—of God—is not so much by knowing it as by *allowing* ourselves to be grasped by it. It's not a mental thing, but a connection that comes by allowing ourselves to be open to God's Spirit.

We sat quietly for a moment. "You know," he finally said, "you and I are lucky."

"Yeah? How's that?"

"We had a wake-up call. An illness. And as you know, the minute you're faced with something like that, everything changes. Suddenly, what held us captive before; the money, the things, judging people, living in the past or the future, wasting time—falls by the wayside. We become keenly aware that our time here on earth is finite. What's most important to us suddenly snaps into focus: our family, our friends, our spirituality, enjoying the simple beauty of nature, a song, or a hug . . . love.

"That façade of pride, arrogance, selfishness—the ego—is stripped away and you're able to glimpse your core essence, your true being . . . that place of God within you . . . "

"So, that God-shaped hole becomes filled?"

"Exactly." Calvin said. "*Fulfilled.*"

chapter 44

evolution of consciousness

The reason it hurts so much to separate is because our souls are connected. Maybe they always have been and always will be.

—ANONYMOUS

We'd been talking for over an hour when Calvin suggested we stretch our legs and get something to drink. "Sure," I said. "I could use some coffee."

We walked quietly down the long staircase, each lost in thought. At the front desk, Calvin informed the receptionist where he was going. Then we began our stroll through the colorful halls of The Factory, back toward The Frisky Berry.

I found myself thinking about the expression *Christ Consciousness*. It was new to me and I wondered exactly what it meant to Calvin.

"For me," he said, "it's about understanding that Heaven is here, and now. We're not separate from God. Sometimes we glimpse it . . . maybe for just a moment. But in that moment we realize how fully connected we are, by the same eternal Christ-Spirit that filled Jesus."

I nodded and smiled. This was something I could relate to. As we walked down the corridor, past restaurants and shops, I told him about my experience as a teenager.

It was the mid-seventies and I'd been invited to a southern-style revival. Raised Episcopalian, this was my first time to a Baptist church. The scene was unforgettable; the hot summer night, the crowded auditorium, and an impassioned preacher moving about the stage. "Je-sus," he bellowed, "is knocking on the door of your heart . . . He paused and whispered, "Will you ask Him in? Will you accept Jesus as your *personal* savior?" It was the classic altar-call. As the congregation sang the old hymn, "Just As I Am," people walked to the front of the stage to dedicate their lives to Christ.

In the balcony, I was frozen in my seat but convicted in my heart. So I made a decision; I would see if Jesus was real. I don't know what I expected, if anything. But as I bowed my head, asking an invisible Jesus into my heart, an amazing thing happened—the floodgates opened to the most incredible kind of love I'd ever felt, and it poured into me. My body seemed to pulsate with light. And, even though I was a teenager, concerned with what others thought, I began crying, sobbing, and thanking God for this very real love. It happened in an instant—my life was changed forever.

Calvin and I stopped outside the coffee shop. "My consciousness," I continued, "went from being unaware of God, to having a real-life relationship with Him. I've struggled with a lot of issues in the thirty-four years since that night, but I've never doubted my relationship with God. I know I'm not alone. He filled that hole in my heart and, whenever I allow Him, He shines through me in the most beautiful ways."

Calvin held the door open for me. "Thanks for sharing that with me, Stowe."

As we waited for the barista at the counter, I asked Calvin if he thought the world in general would ever evolve into a state of Christ Consciousness.

"I believe humanity is heading that way," he said. "It's evolving in science and technology . . . organizational systems, information systems, really everything . . . "

Calvin placed our order. "I think it comes from our developing awareness, of everything and everyone around us. We aren't stuck in caves anymore. We're flying high above it all, where we can see what God has made. We're evolving.

"You know," he continued, "none of this is random. I absolutely believe in an Intelligent Designer. And the more we're influenced by his intelligence, through his Mind or Spirit, the more we develop and evolve into Christ-like and compassionate beings. Of course, we may still be warring and selfish, but I think there's been an awful lot of inspired development in the past 2,000 years too."

We picked up our drinks, wandered back into the hallway, and sat on an old pew. I watched some people walking past. "How do you see humankind evolving?"

Calvin pushed his lips together and took a breath. "I think it happens on two levels; first, as individuals seeking God on their own, and then globally, which I think you can measure as civilizations become more advanced in the pursuits of freedom, equality, and human rights. Either way, I think it leads to a spiritual evolution. And maybe someday we'll hit critical mass and experience a leap in consciousness . . . I don't really know."

"Maybe," I shook my head, "there's still a lot of *stuck* in the *mud* thinking going on."

"Well, there is . . . " He blew on his coffee and took a sip. "But in our information age things can happen suddenly. Take for instance the four-minute mile. For years it was believed to be impossible for a human to run a mile in under four minutes. Then along came Roger Bannister in 1954 . . . he broke it. And he didn't just break a physical barrier, but a *psychological* barrier. After that—it was amazing—lots of people were able to run a mile in under four-minutes. It shows the power of suggestion. Originally it was suggested no one could break it. Once it was broken though, the suggestion was that anyone could. It wasn't a sudden leap in human evolution, it was a leap in human consciousness."

"So where do you imagine this evolution of consciousness will bring us?"

Calvin shrugged. "Back to the Father's house, perhaps? And maybe I should add Mother's too. I say that because the loving and more feminine quality of God's Spirit needs to be part of human development. We've been a male-dominated society for too long. It started as a necessity to protect the family, to go out and kill the beast for food. But it led to a strong, male ego-centered industrial age and commercial era . . . and all that aggression has brought us to a very dangerous place."

Calvin stretched back on the bench. "Fortunately, I think this is changing. We're regaining more of a balance between the masculine and feminine qualities—kind of like the right-brain and left-brain harmonizing. I think the world needs more of the loving and motherly instincts. And the aggressive male tendencies need to lovingly acknowledge that spiritual balance, as in a good marriage . . . like yours and Peter's."

That made me smile. "Thank you."

"Funny . . . " he went on, "the Shakers of last century were aware of that verse in Genesis, *God created man in his own image . . . male and female he created them.* They embraced the idea that God's image was expressed as male and female. And I've read that in ancient Hebrew Scriptures, the Holy Spirit was given the feminine gender[x], like nouns do in French. So I think of God as Father—the masculine, assertive Creator and provider; and the Spirit as having the feminine qualities of an intuitive and healing nurturer, like with a mothers' love. Probably sounds heretical, but the Trinity is always a mystical, mysterious concept; Father, Son, and what . . . Mother? Holy Spirit—maybe that is more feminine, who knows?

"These days, Noetic Science and other fields are saying that when we quiet down our aggressive side, we can tap into such qualities as nonlocal information or, in other words, 'intuition.' Women are better at this than men, so I think it would bring about more balance in the making of world decisions."

I asked if he felt humanity was developing into a more spiritually balanced partnership of male and female traits.

"Maybe." He nodded. "Of course, it's more complicated than just a woman and man being equal. Each person has to balance his or her own male and female qualities. Some men have a well-developed nurturing side, while some women have a strong logical and assertive side. I believe Marilyn and I are each well balanced that way and it makes for a strong partnership."

As Calvin and I got up and walked back to the office, I thought about my own marriage, how Peter enjoyed cooking and I gravitated toward tools and fixing things. It was a good blend and whether we were collaborating on books, films, or building a home and family, it worked for us. We would agree on a goal, then divide and conquer according to our abilities.

I glanced around. The wood, the metal, the decorations, and the stores—everything that makes The Factory special—is the result of two very different people. It made me wonder about Marilyn and Calvin's collective purpose in life.

He paused thoughtfully. "I'd say my purpose—and I believe hers as well—is to move toward that Christ Consciousness, or source consciousness . . . whatever you want to label it. That is our main purpose."

Christ consciousness. We hadn't strayed far from that subject. I was suddenly reminded of a Bible quote. "Do you know in Philippians where Paul says, *Let the same mind be in you that was in Christ Jesus?* That's really what we're talking about, isn't it?"

"Yes," he said, then added, "And do you remember how Jesus often talked about the *Kingdom of Heaven?* "

"Yes, constantly."

Calvin held his right hand out. "He says, 'The Kingdom of Heaven is like this,' and then," holding out his left hand, "'the Kingdom of Heaven is like that' . . . and I don't think he is talking about a place you go to, because he finally just comes right out and says— "

"The Kingdom of Heaven is *within you.*"

"Right!" Calvin grinned. "I think it's a state of *consciousness.* Like you said, we need to put on the mind of Christ. When we have that kind of awareness, we see there is no separation. We're not separate from God or one another."

"*I am the vine . . . And you are the branches.*"

"Exactly," he said. "Jesus makes it clear—we are all connected."

"So, how is it, that most of the time we feel so disconnected from each other? And from God?"

Calvin shook his head. We entered his office and sat down. For a moment we said nothing.

Finally I spoke. "That sense of separateness goes away for me when I get quiet . . . "

Calvin folded his hands and listened.

"The other day," I continued, "I took a few minutes to pray. I started by thanking God . . . and then . . . I got carried away. I started thanking Him for everything I could think of. Past *and* present. Then something strange happened . . . My body started vibrating. It felt electrical. And the more thankful I was, the stronger it got. It seemed like maybe ten minutes had passed. But when I opened my eyes, I'd been there for forty-five minutes!"

"Sounds like you were really in the Spirit."

"I felt like it. And afterwards it occurred to me that the events of the past few years—which I also feel thankful for—have brought about so many important changes in my life." I took a deep breath. "I have more gratitude now. And I feel like I've been able to shift my focus from fear to love. Also, I've seen that the *perfect me* isn't something I need to create—God's already done that. I just need to relax into who He created me to be. All of this makes me feel more willing to place myself in His hands, and . . . " I smiled, "that makes me feel connected."

He nodded, and again we sat in silence.

I glanced over at Calvin's airplane clock, the one with the propeller hands. It was a little after eleven. I knew he needed to get home and let his dogs out, so I gathered my computer and purse. He came around the desk for a farewell hug.

"You know," I said. "I just want tell you that writing this book with you has meant so much to me . . . It's been difficult . . . " I felt my eyes tearing up. "And there were times when I didn't even know if I could go on with it. But it always felt like the right thing to do. And I can see now how the Spirit was working through it all along."

Calvin stood there, quietly. "It's been a journey, hasn't it?"

"Yes."

"I think this was all intended," he said. "It was something we needed to do together . . . something to learn from."

I walked toward the door, then turned around one last time. "If you had a prayer for the book, what would it be?"

Without skipping a beat he closed his eyes, "*May the words of my mouth and the meditations of my heart be acceptable in thy sight, O, Lord, my strength and my redeemer . . . *"

chapter 45

ready to fly

I believe you should live each day as if it is your last.
Which is why I don't have any clean laundry, because, come on,
who wants to do laundry on the last day of their life?

—A Wise Guy

*I*t was a hot June morning and as I stepped onto the north shore of beautiful
Lake Tahoe, I felt a wave of excitement. Our family vacation was suddenly
turning into an opportunity for me to do something I'd often talked about but,
so far, been too afraid to do—fly. My family, including Peter, Christina, Grace,
and my cousin, Clare, followed close behind as I sprinted across the sun-baked
sand to my destination—a small stand with a multi-colored umbrella.

"Good-morning," I said. The young guy manning the stand tossed his
bangs to one side and stood up.

"You here to go parasailing?"

"Yes, sir." I gazed out at the clear blue waters. Across the lake I spotted
a speedboat pulling a big yellow parachute with two people hanging from
it. They seemed like dots floating effortlessly against the blue backdrop. I
turned back to the young man. He asked if I was going alone. I nodded.
"It's just me."

He peered over the stand, giving me the once over. "Uh, there's a two hundred pound minimum." He shook his head. "I'm guessing you don't weight that much. Is there anyone else who could go with you?"

I turned to my girls. I knew they were both scared of heights but I asked anyway. "Do either of you want to go up with me?" They stared back with wide eyes.

Christina was quietly terrified.

"Well, I'd like to . . . " Grace scrunched her face. "But it's looks so high."

"I know it does." I glanced up at the parasailers. "I'm nervous too. That's why I'm going up there—to face my fear." I searched their young eyes. "So who's with me?"

My cousin, Clare, who has been like a sister to me, raised her hand. "If no one else wants to go, I'll do it."

"Really?" I was touched. "You'd do that . . . for me?"

"Only if the girls don't want to."

I turned back to Christina and Grace. Their adolescent faces were twisted with the turmoil of their decision. "Okay," I rubbed my hands together. "Who's it gonna be?" They looked at one another. Of the two, I figured maybe Grace would volunteer. I never expected the answer I got.

Grace stepped forward. "I'll go, Mama."

"Me, too!" Christina chimed in.

My eyes widened. "Both of you? Are you sure?"

They nodded. "Okay," I said. "Let's go!"

Moments later, we bounced across the waves with the cool wind in our hair, laughing nervously as Peter documented our every move with the home-video camera. Out in the middle of the lake, the crew outfitted us with life preservers and a harness. We were ready to fly.

I felt surprisingly peaceful as we sat on the back of the boat waiting for lift-off. Then the powerful twin engines revved up, and I felt my adrenaline kick in. As the boat surged ahead, I noticed we were all white-knuckling the straps that held us.

∞ flying high ∞

All at once, we slid off the back of the boat. "Shockeys, ho!" I yelled. We immediately rose into the cloudless sky.

For a moment everything around us was a blur. We were being pulled outward, upward at a dramatic rate of speed, leaving the boat and our family behind. Down below, Clare waved enthusiastically. We communicated the only way we could—with kicking legs and waving arms. The rumble of the loud motorboat faded, replaced by the whooshing of wind in our ears. We were high and, in a way, helpless, dangling like an eagle's prey far above the water. All we could do was laugh and scream with the excitement of the moment.

Higher and higher we went. Six hundred, seven hundred, eight hundred, and finally—our destination—nine hundred feet in the air.

I could not deny the spectacular view—the snow-capped mountains in the distance, the deep blue of Lake Tahoe, the wonder of the earth far below. Yet, there was something about being up so high that drew me inward. I was magnetized to the moment. Looking at the girls, I suddenly felt like an observer, as if I was a cloud floating by—casually watching the three of us.

Are we actually here? I reached out to touch Christina's back—she was trembling. Then, I laid my hand on Grace's shoulder—she was bouncing. I took a deep breath. Yes, we are here. High above it all. Having fun. And, most of all, still together.

How different things could have been . . . only a few months ago I was about as low a person could be. Bedridden from pain, not only was I depressed, I was dying. In fact, this trip for a family wedding had seemed like an impossibility. Back then, it appeared more likely there would be another kind of family gathering—one where people wear black rather than white. Where, instead of raising champagne glasses and making toasts, they give eulogies and lower their heads. And, in place of celebrations, tears . . .

I shook my head, trying to dislodge the thought of what seemed like a lifetime ago.

We had come so far from those difficult days. I leaned back into my harness. There was no pain in my body. And looking at the girls, I realized, no pain of loss. I put my right arm out like a wing, threw my head back, and yelled, "Whoo hoo!"

Up here, up high, our conversations were sporadic. There was no need for words. We were connected by the racing of our hearts, the shivers down our back. The view was exhilarating, and I listened with satisfaction to the squeals of my girls as we floated up above the evergreens, above the sandy beaches, above the boats, above the clear blue waters, and most of all, above the fear that could have kept us earthbound.

I closed my eyes. Alive and in the moment, I knew without a doubt from where my breath came and I thanked God for it. A verse came to me: But they that wait upon the Lord shall renew their strength; they shall mount up with wings as eagles . . .

All things of this world have their time and our moment of flying was soon over. Yes, it was exciting. I got out of my comfort zone and did the thing I feared. Now, with that elevated perspective Calvin talks about, I found myself ready to return to earth, to begin anew.

They were reeling us in, lower and lower, until we were just above the water. They slowed the boat, allowing us to drift down just enough so we could splash our feet in the lake. I felt the pull of gravity as we hit the cold waters of Tahoe. Then, whoosh! We were airborne again, headed for the cruiser.

Grace was beaming. "You know, I was scared before . . . " She leaned forward in her harness and kicked her legs. "but now I want to do it again!"

I laughed. "Me too."

As we came in at a forty-five degree angle, legs dangling, I noticed Peter documenting our flight from the front of the vessel. Coming closer, I could see the others cheering. We were right above the surface of the white-capped wake. The man on the deck tried calling to us over the roar of the engine. "Put your legs down!"

I thought he said to put our legs out, so I held mine straight in front of me. "No," he called once more. "Put your legs DOWN!" As I did, they revealed something that caught my eye: two words printed on the transom of the boat. I was about to return safely to the vessel named Flying High.

A year had passed since I wrote the opening lines of this book.

Flying high . . . it's the song of birds, music played by wings on the wind, soaring through the skies. For them, flying is as natural as breathing. They were born to it.

For a lot of folks flying high means freedom from the gravity of fear, a chance to soar into the blue vastness of life's possibilities, to look at clouds from the other side and, to see with heightened awareness a panoramic view of God's creation . . .

A lot has happened to me since I first wrote those words. I think back sometimes at the person I was then. How tentative I was about life. And living. I had a definite fear of heights but, more than that, I had a fear of falling. Of failing. It's possible I might have stayed that way, never going beyond my imagined boundaries for the rest of my life. But somewhere deep down inside, I suppose, I knew that was unacceptable. As Calvin often says, "I can do better than that."

So, consciously or not, I believe I drew to myself a mentor who could gently nudge me from the safety of my nest. And as I rose above my doubts and fears, I was suddenly elevated to a place of openness, of hope and trust that I was exactly where God wanted me to be. And it was there in the stillness of my soul that I could, at long last, hear the song in my heart.

I used to fly only in my dreams. Now I have flown beyond my wildest dreams. I have stood with the sun on my shoulders, spread my wings, and caught the breeze that lifts me toward the crystal heavens—where my spirit longs to be.

Flying high. No, it's not just for birds and the brave. I believe it's what we were all meant to do. Maybe that's why we're drawn to those who conquer new heights, those who dare to rise above it all. We want to be like them. We want to fly too . . .

letter to calvin

Dear Calvin,

As our project comes to an end, it seems natural to write a letter of thanks . . . with that 'attitude of gratitude' you always talk about. I am grateful, not only for your friendship, but for all you taught and all the faith you've shown.

We've come a long way since we first decided to chronicle your experiences. We started as strangers with a common vision. But we needed to get to know one another. So we began meeting on Mondays—in your office, out at your farm, and various landmarks along your life's path. In the beginning, I figured you would talk, I would write. But the more I listened, the more I learned, and

the more I wanted to know. Through this sharing, the teacher and the student became friends.

I looked forward to Monday mornings. No topic
was off-limits; personal victories; struggles;
dreams; or discoveries. We shared the stories of
life. Seasons changed, challenges arose, and new
stories were born. We became fellow travelers,
celebrating, commiserating, and sharing hope.

I learned from you, both in person and from
the seminar tapes you made earlier in your career.
As I transcribed those words, I felt the excitement of a young teacher giving firsthand accounts
of the power of one's thoughts. Your mission and
message were clear: to motivate others to realize
their full potential, which their Creator intended
for them. You pushed them to rise above their
fears. "What would you do," you asked with genuine interest, "if you knew you could not fail?"

You followed your own dreams, experienced
life's fears and rose above them. You struggled,
as all humans do, within the limitations and
hardships of our earthly home, yet managed to
keep a positive outlook. You proved that, when
pursuing dreams, you can't always believe what
you see-you have to believe what you feel.

You are an eternal seeker and I love how you
embrace your own faith, while respecting the

beliefs of others. A verse from the poem, The Blind Men and the Elephant, sums up your view of how we each perceive God.

> "So oft in theologic wars,
> The disputants, I ween,
> Rail on in utter ignorance
> Of what each other mean,
> And prate about an Elephant
> Not one of them has seen!"[xi]

You encouraged me to connect with God, quiet my mind, and let life flow. To believe beyond my doubt, and use with abandon, the talents I've been given. I learned that it's not about me. It's not how well I sing or play or write. It's about how God uses those gifts to minister to others.

You reminded me that the best things in this life are free—our thoughts, health, family, friends, a sunny day, and the companionship of a devoted pet . . . just a few of the things money can't buy. They are simply gifts from our Creator.

I thought transcribing your life story would only take a few months. Then life happened, and my health declined. There were times I wasn't productive. You could have given up on me, but you didn't. Even when I thought I was dying (and might not finish our book) you showed patience I did not expect. You reminded me of my freedom to make choices, whatever they were. You never lost faith in my recovery, or showed concern about our unfinished work. And because you often have an elevated perspective, your encouragement and support frequently lifted me when I needed it most.

So how, I wonder, will I thank you?

I'll begin by being a brighter light in this world. By singing the songs in my heart. By choosing my words more carefully. By remembering to give thanks for everything-even the hardships. As I walk through the adversities of this world, I'll look for those "seeds of greatness."

I will strive to love others, and give more than expected. Instead of clenching my hands, I will open them to share my resources, my love, and my time. I've heard, "Love is paying attention." In order to truly love, we must be present, and listen with our hearts. That is where we must hold one another, for when someone is in your heart-no matter what happens-they are never really gone.

Proverbs 17:17 says," A friend loveth at all times."

Thanks, Calvin, for being my friend.

With love,
Stowe

Everything will be okay in the end.
And if it's not okay, it's not the end.
—Anonymous

· ·

acknowledgements

from Stowe

I would like to thank Angela and Dan DePriest, our editors, for their wisdom and encouragement; Clare Novak for generously helping me sort through the chaos to find the "seeds of greatness;" Rita Davenport for her enthusiasm; Jean Bertram, Rita Brockman, Mary Belle Browder, Terri Clement, Bob Clement, Liz Foster, Christine Katcher, Matthew Katcher, Marilyn LeHew, Mary Jane McClarty, Donna Scott, Gene Smith, and Lisa Tichenor for giving these pages an early read and lending their insights. Special thanks to our church family and all those who prayed for me during my illness; Judy McDonald and Lynee Lane for always being there; Christina and Grace for loving me through a debilitating disease and then sharing me with my laptop; and especially to Peter—without you, this book would not exist. I am grateful for your thoughts, insights, and patience. My appreciation to Calvin LeHew for sharing his story with me. And, finally, I thank God for a *second chance* to live.

from Calvin

My thanks to Rita Davenport for her friendship and encouragement in writing this book; to Rod Pewitt and the staff at The Factory for their dedicated service; to my mother and father in memory of their guidance; to Marilyn for not only faithfully accompanying me on many high adventures, but also helping me land on my feet. And thanks especially, to my Creator.

Also by Calvin LeHew
Manifesting Dreams
Miss Daisy's Cookbook (Recipes from Miss Daisy's)
Choice's Cookbook (Choice Recipes from Choice's Restaurant)

Also by Stowe and Peter Shockey
Reflections of Heaven
The Hallelujah Diet
The Hallelujah Diet Workbook
Journey of Light
Angel Stories—DVD
Stories of Miracles—DVD
Life After Life—DVD

For more information on *Life After Life* film, go to:
www.LifeAfterLifeTV.com

LOOK FOR THESE AND OTHER TITLES AT:
www.OutsideTheBlox.com

about the authors

CALVIN LEHEW is a lifelong visionary and currently the owner of The Factory At Franklin, an eclectic shopping and learning center. He has been President of the Williamson County Chamber of Commerce, co-founder of the Downtown Franklin Association, President of the Natchez Trace Parkway Association just to name a few. He served on the President's Commission on White House Fellowship and is an animal rights supporter and leader in his community. He is also a motivational speaker and author of *Manifesting Dreams*. He lives with his wife and two dogs in Franklin, Tennessee.

STOWE DAILEY SHOCKEY is a gifted singer and songwriter, having written music with Garth Brooks, Shenandoah (she had the title cut on their album *Long Time Comin'*) and many others in the Nashville music community. Her album, *Angel Chants*, was the inspirational sound track of *Angel Stories*, featured on The Learning Channel. She is also a volunteer music therapist for Alive Hospice. Together, with her husband Peter, she has co-authored five books, including *Journey of Light*, the story of her own troubled childhood. She lives outside of the Nashville area with her husband and two daughters.

PLEASE SEND THOUGHTS OR COMMENTS TO:

Stowe@FlyingHighBook.com

FOR MORE INFORMATION GO TO:

www.FlyingHighBook.com
www.FlyingHighFilm.com
www.OutsideTheBlox.com

Outside The BLOX Media
PO Box 864, Franklin, TN 37065

VISIT THE FACTORY IN FRANKLIN TENNESSEE:

www.FactoryAtFranklin.com

i.   Earl Nightingale, *The Strangest Secret*, Audible Audio Edition, Earl Nightingale, July 2010.

ii. Gregg Braden, *The Spontaneous Healing of Belief*, Hay House, 2008.

iii. Danny E. Morris, *A Life That Really Matters*, Tidings, 1968.

iv. Ernest Holmes, *The Science of Mind: A Philosophy, A Faith, A Way of Life*, The Definitive Edition, Tarcher Putnam, 1998

v. ibid.

vi. Alana Stewart, David Kessler, *My Journey with Farrah: A Story of Life, Love, and Friendship*, William Morrow, 2009.

vii. Gerald W. Barrax, *Another Kind of Rain: Fourth Dance Poem*, University of Pittsburgh Press, 1970

viii. David Richo, *The Power of Coincidence: How Life Shows Us What We Need to Know*, Shambhala, 2007.

ix. ibid.

x. http://www.truthortradition.com/iphone/index.php?option=com_content&view=article&id=111:gods-gift-of-holy-spirita-he-or-an-it-&catid=39:gift-of-holy-spirit&Itemid=61 (see parag 9).

xi. John Godfrey Saxe, *The Poems of John Godfrey Saxe: The Blind Men and the Elephant*. Boston: Houghton, Mifflin and Company, 1881.